MODERN ECONOMIC ISSUES

OTTO ECKSTEIN, Harvard University, General Editor

In this series the great public issues in economics are posed and put in perspective by original commentary and reprints of the most interesting and significant recent statements by experts in economics and government.

STANLEY LEBERGOTT, the editor of this volume, has dealt with the problem of unemployment as a consultant with the U.S. Department of Labor and a member of the Board of Directors of the Social Science Research Council. Presently the chairman of the Department of Economics at Wesleyan University, Professor Lebergott is the author of numerous articles on unemployment and the book, *Manpower in Economic Growth: The American Record Since 1800.*

MEN WITHOUT WORK

THE ECONOMICS OF UNEMPLOYMENT

Edited by Stanley Lebergott

PRENTICE-HALL, Inc., Englewood Cliffs, N.J.
A SPECTRUM BOOK

Current printing (last digit):
11 10 9 8 7 6 5 4 3 2

CONTENTS

v

Over here freedom means hard wurruk. What is th' am-
bition iv all iv us, Hinnissy? 'Tis ayether to hold our job
or to get wan. We want wurruk. We must have it. D'ye
raymimber th' sign th' mob carrid in th' procession las'
year? "Give us wurruk, or we perish," it said. They had
their heads bate in be polismen because no philan-
thropist'd come along an' make thim shovel coal. . . .

Mr. Dooley in Peace and in War,
F. P. Dunne

INTRODUCTION

UNEMPLOYMENT: A PERSPECTIVE

Stanley Lebergott

A week before Christmas in 1819, the polished, astute and wealthy leader of the "dismal science" of economics, David Ricardo, rose in Parliament to oppose that durable visionary, Robert Owen. "It could not be denied on the whole view of the subject," Ricardo declared, "that machinery did *not* lessen the demand for labor." [1] Saying so, he voiced the accepted wisdom of economists and entrepreneurs, of that time and (to a marvelous extent) of the years since.

Yet surely the hand-weavers must have found that statement absurd, idled in a winter of discontent brought on by the new machine looms. But Ricardo went on to note—in almost the words of Walter Reuther a century and a half later—that "on the other hand . . . [machinery] did not consume the produce of the soil, nor employ any of our factory workers." * Indeed he found it quite obvious that "the extensive use of machinery, by throwing a large portion of labour into the market, while on the other hand, there might not be a corresponding increase of demand for it, must in some degree, operate prejudicially to the working classes." Yet, "he would not tolerate any law to prevent the use of machinery." Why not? Because even "if they gave up a system which enabled them to undersell in the foreign market, would other nations refrain from pursuing it? Certainly not." England was "therefore bound, for its own interest, to continue it." [2]

In a later, more pungent statement, Philip Wicksteed wrote:

If all the world turned sober, it would indefinitely increase its well-being, but countless publicans, brewers, distillers, and hop- and vine-

---

* Presumbaly apocryphal, the story states that Reuther was shown around a fully automatic plant by a management man who remarked: "these machines don't pay union dues," to which Reuther replied: "And they won't buy cars either."

1

growers would be thrown out of employment. If universal peace were secured, and armaments were reduced to the vanishing point, there would be many an Othello to mourn that his occupation was gone. If a really successful unpuncturable tyre were put on the market, there would be a great increase in collective happiness . . . . profanity, at least in cultivated society, would tend to be more closely restricted to its natural preserves on the golf-links, but there would be a procession of unemployed . . . bicycle repairers. . . .

Thus every man who lives by supplying any want, dreads anything which tends either to dry up that want or to supply it more easily and abundantly. . . .[3]

Man versus machine; harsh conclusions (in which economists seem to delight) versus the hopes of humanity—these apparent conflicts have continued to our own day. True, the problems of unemployment dwindled during the boom decade 1946-56. But since then a shadow has fallen—dark in itself, and menacing in its implications. In only three of the seventy-two months from 1958 through 1963 did the U.S. unemployment rate run below 5 per cent, seasonally adjusted. Perhaps even more worrisome is the fact that it rarely rose above 6 per cent during the same period, for so narrow a range suggests that we have moved into an underemployment equilibrium. If so, the economy might be normally geared to an unemployment rate over 5 per cent—with 2 million more jobless workers than if we held to, say, a 3.5 per cent minimum.

To distinguish fear from fact and to determine what must be done, it is first necessary to analyze recent U.S. experience, to test that experience against the basic forces that bring resource idleness. This volume begins with a review of some of the major open issues. (The section thus serves to introduce the conflicting viewpoints of the later articles.) The first issue it takes up is an apparently simple one: Who are the unemployed?* Who is included in our measures of unemployment; and who ought to be included? Clearly, the

* The reader who thinks the question a simple or trivial one need only refer to a 1963 article in a distinguished magazine (by a leading economist) which stated that "in the U.S. two distinct series of unemployment statistics are produced by the Bureau of Employment Statistics and the Census. The discrepancies between these series are enormous. The BES series has averaged lower than that of the Census in every year but 1946." The objection is equivalent to saying that there were enormous discrepancies in every year since 1947 between the number of Princeton graduates and the number of Ivy League graduates.

answer will challenge any evaluation of our unemployment problem—its nature, its potential solutions, how it compares with that
of other nations.

Second, what are the characteristics of the unemployed? They are
not identical nor do they subsist on an equal level of want and hopelessness. But the range in their characteristics will affect the power
of market forces to reduce unemployment significantly, as well as
the success of policy actions designed to cut it down. We suggest
some more hopeful (and contentious) conclusions on the meaning
of these differences in unemployment rates by color, region, and skill
levels than many accepted structural analyses imply. (The articles
by Zeisel and Stein provide succinct, up-to-date reviews of the statistics on such differences.)

We turn then to the lively and much debated issue: Is there a
new unemployment problem? Does the unemployment problem in
recent years differ significantly from that in the past? Will the traditional remedies be effective? And what about the effect of automation on the level of joblessness? Does it portend a drastic and
hopeless change for the worse? (Killingsworth, Heller, and Brozen
reflect the opposed positions on this question.)

Finally, we turn to two major policy questions: Given recent
U.S. experience, what can the nation seek as a reasonable unemployment minimum? How do we evaluate the major solutions suggested in recent Congressional hearings, executive reports and
legislative acts designed to solve the present unemployment problem? (This discussion leads into a look at U.S. and foreign policies,
as covered in the articles by Somers, Uhr, and the Joint Economic
Committee.)

WHO ARE THE UNEMPLOYED?

How serious a nation's unemployment problem is will be fixed by
the size and composition of the group it includes in the unemployment total. If a worker must get permission before leaving his job
(or suffer a penalty)—as was the case in the Soviet Union in 1940-56
—the nation will report little or no unemployment.[4] When such
restrictions are lifted, unemployment appears, of course.* If, as in

* The labor turnover rate in Soviet manufacturing in 1958-60 ran about
40 per cent, and the duration of unemployment for those leaving averaged
about one month. *Monthly Labor Review* (January 1962), 18.

Italy, the law stipulates the terms under which an employee can be fired, requires dismissal pay, and establishes a set of legal councils to determine which firings are without "just cause," then a nation's unemployment total will surely be lower than if it followed U.S. job-market procedures.[5] Japan, for instance, has notably low unemployment rates because some 40 per cent of its manufacturing employees apparently have what amount to lifetime tenure.[6] And if a nation is largely rural, its unemployment will have low visibility. For unemployment's close equivalent—pitifully low productivity, will be concealed in the form of "disguised unemployment" on many a family farm, and in the host of small bazaar and marketing activities. Recent estimates for Indonesia, for example, report only 1.5 per cent of the labor force unemployed—but 40-60 per cent in disguised unemployment.[7] The very nature of "unemployment in a backward area is a phenomenon radically different from that which it appears to be in an advancing economy."[8] For it carries implications of a permanent hopelessness and a disorganization of both economic activity and familial life.

Even where free labor markets and urban employment characterizes the nation, one may still define *unemployment* in a variety of ways. Some countries with broadly comprehensive unemployment insurance systems use registration for insurance benefits to measure unemployment. Unfortunately such a measure usually fails to indicate the full extent of unutilized manpower or of need. Waiting periods, exemptions, failure to qualify, and exhaustion of benefits typically distort the use of insurance service figures for such purposes. It is for such reasons that a number of nations (including some with comprehensive insurance coverage) have set up labor force unemployment sample surveys on the U.S. model.

Since 1940 U.S. unemployment estimates have been provided in full and reliable detail from the Monthly Survey of the Labor Force, conducted by the Bureau of the Census and published by the Bureau of Labor Statistics.* For the survey week (taken to reflect conditions in the month) everyone aged fourteen and older is clas-

---

* Issued in special releases, these data can most conveniently be consulted in two U.S. Bureau of Labor Statistics monthly publications: *Employment and Earnings* and the *Monthly Labor Review*. Summary data from the survey appear annually in the *Economic Report of the President,* and monthly in the *Survey of Current Business* and the *Federal Reserve Bulletin.*

sified as either in the labor force or out of it. Persons are classified in the labor force if they report themselves in one of the two segments that make it up—the employed, and the unemployed.* The "employed" includes anyone who has worked in any part of the survey week: the teen-ager who babysits for one hour for pay is classed as employed. So is the man who began work at nine on Monday morning, was fired at ten, and has been without a job ever since.** So too are those workers idled by bad weather, strikes, or illness. We adopt so comprehensive a definition of employment in order to accept the full evidence of what the market indicates to be employment. (The national product of a country is also measured comprehensively: it includes spending for liquor and good books, for modern art and automobiles with fins. Each item utilizes resources, each finds a market. As such it is simply included in our output total.)

Similarly the labor force survey makes no distinction among the abilities, interests, competence, zeal, or extent of work of the employed. Obviously we do want to know about such distinctions. Hence the survey also provides separate figures for the number of people working under fifteen hours in the survey week, the number of teen-agers at work, the number of people employed in domestic service, and so on.

The same principle of comprehensiveness governs the measurement of unemployment. The unemployment total includes "all persons who did not work at all during the survey week and were looking for work, regardless of whether or not they were eligible for unemployment insurance." Eligibility for unemployment insurance is not used as a criterion because some unemployed are not in activities covered by social insurance (e.g., farming, domestic service); because others have not been unemployed long enough to qualify for insurance payments; and because still others exhaust

---

* To achieve reliability in reporting, the survey asks about activity in the week preceding that in which it is taken each month. The week thus is taken as an adequate sample of the average level of labor force, employment, and unemployment during the month. Many of the central problems in labor force definition are outlined in Louis Ducoff and Margaret Hagood, *Labor Force Definition and Measurement* (1947).

** The Gordon Committee Report (p. 46) indicated that as of February 1961, 940,000 persons were included in the employment total (of 64,655,000) because they had worked between one and four hours during the survey week.

their benefits during prolonged periods of joblessness.* Given the many ways in which people seek work, the survey must also include as unemployed

. . . those who did not work at all and (a) were waiting to be called back to a job from which they had been laid off; or (b) were waiting to report to a new wage or salary job within 30 days (and were not in school during the survey week); or (c) would have been looking for work except that they were temporarily ill or believed no work was available in their line of work or in the community. Persons in the latter category will usually be residents of a community in which there are only a few dominant industries which were shut down during the survey week.[9]

Those on temporary layoff—group (a) above—must be included because they, like the other unemployed, were looking for work in the survey week. (They, of course, were restricting their search to the job from which they had been laid off). The survey focuses on current activity: neither the survey nor the laid-off worker is sufficiently clairvoyant to know whether he will actually return to work or when that will be. American industry typically tries to keep workers on the payroll (by means of temporary layoff and work-sharing) before resorting to outright firing. Hence such layoffs are a significant factor in the labor market and a common form of unemployment. (This, of course, has an exact parallel in the treatment of employment: the person who works at a short time job during the survey week is defined as employed, even though he may prove to be jobless the next week. Since these data are designed to compare the amount and trend of employment with those of unemployment, the criteria used to define each group must be similar.[10])

It will be noted that all those classified as unemployed must be seeking work—an activity that ranges from checking with employed workers, to applying at a factory gate or checking advertisements.**

---

* If the necessary adjustments could be made for these conceptual differences, however, it seems likely that the two series would give the same evidence in the course of recession and recovery. The major feasible adjustments are made, and the close similarity for 1954-61 indicated, in the Gordon Report, Chap. 4.

** For a typical description of job-search procedures, *see* the statement from L. P. Adams and R. L. Aronson, *Workers and Industrial Change: A Case*

The group, however, also includes those who "were temporarily ill or believed no work was available in their line of work or in their community." Miners in a small coal mining town who do want to work know that they will learn so promptly when the mine reopens that it is pointless for them to look for work actively.*

It has been proposed to include within the unemployed group only male heads of families, on the assumption that it is this group alone that constitutes a significant problem. Isn't the joblessness of a man of forty-five with four children much more serious than that of a teen-ager or a married woman whose husband does have a job?

Inasmuch as the survey data do provide sufficient detail on the contribution to total unemployment changes made by each of the major groups—according to age, sex, and marital status—such a proposal is really concerned not with lack of knowledge but with the analytic limitations of an aggregate measure.

It is important to note, however, that the criteria for unemployment must be similar to those for employment. Thus if single women are to be excluded from unemployment totals, they must be excluded from the employment aggregates as well. The resultant trend in the unemployment rate, however, is going to look much the same as it did before such exclusion.**

But there is a more vital objection: in a free labor market, no group of unemployed can be ignored as adventitious or irrelevant. In many low-income families, the wife and children work to bring family income up to a tolerable level. Suppose such workers were to be excluded—not merely from the survey, but from the labor force itself? Both public-relief spending and wage rates for unskilled male workers would tend to jump to compensate for the loss of family income. The actual labor market process in the United States

---

Study of Labor Mobility (1957) p. 155: "Workers in Auburn, when they become unemployed . . . are in the habit of finding work mainly by direct application at plant employment offices or through tips and information from friends, relatives, and former employers."

* The possibility that others look for work but do not volunteer that fact—and hence are excluded from the official unemployment series—is considered in the President's Committee *Report,* p. 50, where it is noted that as of August 1955 about a million people were classed as not in the labor force but had actually looked for work during the prior two months.

** Data by marital status are shown in the Annual Reports—e.g., U.S. Bureau of Labor Statistics Special Labor Force Report No. 31; *Labor Force and Employment, 1960-62.*

always involves a higher level of labor force participation by members of families the heads of which are unskilled, rural, nonwhite, or disabled. Such participation is also affected by unemployment in families at all income levels. (Fire an account executive of an advertising agency, or a construction laborer, and you are going to induce his wife and teen-age children to search for work—i.e., to become "unemployed" in order to supplement family income.) So long, therefore, as the economy does operate in this fashion, we are not well advised to put on blinders, deciding that we wish to know about only a portion of the labor market process. Instead we must comprehend all those employed and all those seeking work. (A full understanding of the changes in the economy of course requires separate study of the impact of unemployment on particular age, color, and occupation groups—as well as of changes in the credit markets, plant capacity, balance of payments and military demands.)

"Unemployables" are not classified as either employed or unemployed—but, rather, as "not in the labor force." Again, this is a matter of individual determination. Just as blind men are employed at jobs for which some laymen would not expect them to be qualified, so are there among the unemployed persons whom some would consider unemployable.* But unless certifying boards are established to determine eligibility for work, we must accept as employed those who are in fact employed, and accept as unemployed those who are seeking work. An actual examination of the data shows that this question becomes unimportant in practice: most persons in the employed and unemployed groups conform to general expectations. However, the typical concern about definitions does help to emphasize the wisdom of looking at the full array of data on the labor force before attempting to assess the significance of the unemployment total.

---

* It is worth remembering the number of publicists in 1945-46 who decided that the postwar labor force could not reach 60 million because such groups as married women, older workers, youngsters, did not "belong" in, and hence would not be in, the labor force. In a free economy it is hard to imagine excluding such groups from participation in the labor force—or excluding them from the statistics on employment and unemployment when they do participate.

UNEMPLOYMENT: CHARACTERISTICS

Differences among the unemployment rates of different groups are one of the more obvious facts of economic life. Analyses of these differences occasionally reach the unpalatable conclusion that some groups are unemployable—per se, or in today's labor market. From this conclusion one or another dubious inference may be drawn: (1) such groups must be miraculously transformed beyond recognition—impossible; (2) the private labor market must be totally reorganized—undesirable; or (3) the unemployment of these groups must be sadly accepted as inevitable. These difficult and unreachable alternatives, however, are false.

"Workers over forty-five years of age have been troubled by special unemployment problems" says a recent study. Of course. But even in the recession year of 1962 over 96 per cent of the workers in this group were employed. "Unemployment has been much heavier among Negro than among white workers." True again. But of the nonwhite men and women in the 1962 labor force, 89 per cent were employed. High unemployment rates among the uneducated and the unskilled did prevail every year from 1958 through 1963; yet in 1963, 90 per cent of the group did find work. An effective solution to the unemployment problem does not require rejuvenating the aged, aging the young, changing the racial heritage of minority groups, or expanding the educational achievement of the entire labor force.

The practical problem is: How shall we deal with marginal persons within these groups—and with the great bulk of the unemployed who are, in fact white, reasonably well educated, and under forty-five? The marginal workers in this dominant group are not there for any simple reason of genetics or prejudice. They are there because at existing pay rates, existing conditions of labor supply and employment, they are on the ragged edge of the labor market. Change any of these conditions and they may (indeed often do) become employed.

Age

A multitude of surveys have reported relatively high unemployment rates for older workers. The high rates pointed to the decline

in abilities of older workers—not in any absolute sense but in relation to what younger workers in the same job markets had to offer
in the way of abilities and the rates of pay sought by both groups.
Several studies have demonstrated that the productivity of a group
of older employees in a given company is equivalent to that of a
group of younger employees in the same company. Such studies
are irrelevant,* for those older workers who do remain employed
(and are therefore available for surveys) are likely to have been
so selected as to offer equivalent productivity. The heavy unemployment among older workers as a group testifies to the likelihood that
those not employed were less productive than younger workers,
given the present organization of industry.**

There is nothing inevitable in such a relationship—as has been
shown by experience since then. In 1931—the pit of the depression—
the Canadian government reported that male earners over sixty-five
typically lost 50 per cent more working time during the year than
those in the prime age groups.[11] By the middle 1950's, however,
the unemployment rates for older workers were no longer greater.
In 1955-60, in fact, they were distinctly lower than those for men
in the prime age groups.[12] And in the United States, the higher
rates shown for oldsters by the 1940 Census have given way, since
World War II, to rates much the same as those for the prime age
groups.[13] A dominant force whittling down the excess in rates
proved to be the creation and expansion of the social security system. The proportion of older men in the labor force declined sharply
in the postwar years. Marginal incomes available to them became
less of an inducement for them to stay in the labor force than the

* One of the most careful recent studies is summarized by Jerome Mark in
"Measurement of Job Performance and Age," *Monthly Labor Review* (December 1956). Although this study notes a decline with age, it concludes that
it "was not of serious proportions." These data do reveal that in fourteen of
the sixteen occupation groupings reported output rates were lower for the
fifty-five to sixty-four group than the thirty-five to fifty-four group. (For six
categories the twenty-five to thirty-four group was also lower.)

** It is better than a fair possibility that some types of retraining, some sets
of new experiences, could neutralize the losses that come with age and make
it possible for the cumulated knowledge and experience of older workers to
operate more tellingly. However the private advantage to any one employer of
achieving this appears to be inadequate to stimulate individual employers to
provide such training.

retirement incomes offered by the social security system were an invitation to leave it. We may infer that the least employable (i.e., most unemployment-prone) took relatively great advantage of the retirement alternative—thus cutting the historic excess of unemployment rates for the older group.

Education

The past decade has seen both an ebullient spread of automated techniques of production and a rise in unemployment rates for the unskilled and the young. It is hardly surprising that some analysts have connected the two, have therefore urged that we increase the level of education to guard against further rises of unemployment. Now it is essential for economic growth, and for truly full employment of resources, for every worker to be highly (and increasingly) productive. But the assumption that an increased level of education will prevent unemployment misapprehends at least one fundamental characteristic of the unemployed.

The unemployed are those who are marginal in the existing state of offer and demand in the labor market. If all workers in the labor force had their education improved (or their pulchritude), some would still be marginal. Their marginality would then appear to be associated with some other simple single characteristic. Or, when the pattern of final demand and costs shifted, people of identical talents would simply be randomly dismissed. Suppose everyone had a Sorbonne doctorate and a law degree plus a full apprenticeship as a machinist. Then, when demand shifted away from the high-cost textile firms, or from American to foreign steel, those who were fired would all turn out to have doctorates, law degrees, and high craft talents. Their ability to get other work would still turn on the pattern of demand in other plants and industries.

It is a sobering thought that recent studies in India show that unemployed workers there "have higher educational status than do the employed. There is some evidence also that the technical qualifications (at least on paper) of the unemployed are somewhat superior to those of the employed. . . . Almost one in three of India's educated unemployed holds university degrees or has passed the intermediate examination in arts, science, or commerce. There

is some evidence . . . that these more educated have been longer
unemployed." In large cities in India literates made up 52 per cent
of the employed—and 78 per cent of the unemployed.[14]

Recent student riots in Korea reflect an enormous flow of students from colleges—for few jobs requiring college training.* A
similar situation appears to have prevailed in a number of leading
central European countries in the 1930's.[15]

High educational levels do not remove workers from the forces
of supply and demand. If there is a large and consistent excess
demand for highly educated workers, then retraining some of the
unemployed (and further training some of the new workers) will
indeed enable them to move into well-paid jobs. This possibility
is, however, not automatically indicated by mere differences in unemployment rates among the different educational levels at any
point in time. Such differences may merely reflect the marginality
of certain groups of workers.

The wisdom of improving and extending the education of the
next generation of workers is another issue. Further study is needed,
however, to determine whether simple extension of formal education is likely to be more effective in minimizing unemployment than
is specific job training, improved job-placement procedures, or some
other combination of alternatives.

Discrimination

The dramatic excess of nonwhite unemployment rates over those
for whites has captured increasing attention in recent years. Perhaps the most typical inference as to its meaning and its implications for policy is implied by the familiar phrase: "last hired, first
fired." The higher rates, according to the *Manpower Report of the
President,* do reflect in part—possibly about half—"the heavy concentration of Negroes in occupations particularly susceptible to
unemployment—unskilled farm and nonfarm labor, semiskilled production jobs, and service occupations." But, the report points out
that "discrimination against nonwhites . . ." is also an obvious factor, in this picture, difficult though it may be to assess precisely.

* *The New York Times* (April 26, 1964) reports 600 of the 31,241 graduates this year finding jobs through open examinations given by government
and some large private enterprises.

Its presence accounts at least in part for the limited access of nonwhite workers to the skilled and professional occupations . . . [and] for their restricted upward movement even within the occupational groups in which they are widely employed.[16]

It is essential for us to distinguish between the forces associated with the entrance of Negroes into certain occupations and those associated with their becoming unemployed. The former involve a variety of social and political factors much broader than the labor market. One may go on to ask, with respect to those forces in the labor market: Do unemployment differentials testify to discrimination? The evidence on this point is far from clear. In 1950, the unemployment rate for nonwhite males was 7.8 per cent—nearly double the 4.6 per cent rate for white males—as compared with 8.8 per cent and 4.6 per cent, respectively, in 1962.[17] Thus the gap between white and nonwhite rates was greater in the recession year of 1962 than the end of recession figure for the Spring of 1950. But the 1950 range is great enough to give us a basis for investigation. Let us look at the contrasting rates for urban areas—nearly 90 per cent of all unemployment being in such areas. The rates, by region, are given in Table 1.*

Table 1

Unemployment rate for males in urban areas, 1950

	Total	Nonwhite	Ratio
Northeast	6.6	12.4	1.87
North Central	4.5	11.0	2.44
South	4.1	8.1	1.97
West	7.1	13.5	1.91

The difference between total rates and nonwhite rates might be taken as a simple indication of discrimination or lack of education. This, however, will not do. The 2:1 ratio for the South may appear as confirmation. But the same ratio, for all practical purposes also appears for the Northeast and West. And the ratio for the North

* *1950 Census of Population*, Vol. II, Part 1: *U.S. Summary*, Table 155. For the South data shown for total refer only to whites. This understates the evidence for the point being made in the text.

Central region is significantly and substantially greater. A similar pattern is found in the 1940 Census figures (Table 2).*

Table 2

Unemployment rate for males in urban areas, 1940

	Total	Nonwhite	Ratio
Northeast	17.8	33.8	1.90
North Central	15.7	35.3	2.25
South	11.4	21.4	1.88
West	15.2	20.7	1.36

Once again the South shows one of the lowest ratios; the North Central region, the highest.[18]

If one seeks to explain white-nonwhite unemployment differentials on the basis of discrimination, then this regional breakdown is surely puzzling. Even if one assumes that discrimination operates in addition through admission to such unemployment-prone occupations as labor and such industries as construction, can this account for the regional patterns? Is discrimination really greater in the North Central region than the South, or the pattern of job entrance for Negroes so different there from that of the other regions in 1937, 1940, and 1950? It seems likely that an additional factor is at work, and one that is more potent in accounting for unemployment differentials than those usually mentioned.

The very high unemployment rates evident not merely for Negroes but for the poorly educated and the unskilled in general are in significant part related to a phenomenon that is usually ignored in this connection. From the end of World War II through 1963 over 16 million farm residents left their farms—most of them, for the city.[19] In Mississippi alone, from 1950 to 1958, 260,000 Negro farmers left their farms, two thirds of them moving to cities.[20] Is it an unreasonable surmise that these migrants lacked a wide range of skills, knowledges, and attitudes requisite for urban jobs? Unfortunately systematic confirmation of this inference is lacking, but detailed data from the 1950 Census permit some comparisons. For example,

* *1940 Census of Population: Employment and Personal Characteristics,* Table 15. We combine data for those on emergency work with those seeking work.

the over-all unemployment rate for men thirty to thirty-four living in the North Central region was 3 per cent—but the rate for those who had migrated from farms was 10 per cent.[21]

The high tide of prosperity and wartime demand displaced millions of persons during World War II. In the postwar period, the restocking of consumer goods, the population boom, and the Cold War production made available opportunities in unprecedented numbers. The result was an upsurge in internal migration—substantially exceeding, during this brief decade and a half, the net intercensus migration during all the decades from General Grant to General Eisenhower.*

Another indication of the impact of migration appears where the issue of discrimination is raised hardly at all. The three major labor market areas in Puerto Rico—Mayaguez, Ponce, and San Juan—maintained among the highest unemployment rates in the nation every year from 1958 to 1962. At the same time their unemployment rates for workers covered by unemployment insurance have been among the lowest in the nation.** The clear inference is that a substantial number of people have entered these urban labor markets recently enough not to have qualified for such insurance. The heavy migration from Puerto Rican underemployment and low-income farms to cities has helped to raise unemployment rates wherever the migrants went—San Juan, Mayaguez, Ponce, and New York City as well.

If therefore we analyze the income and opportunity differentials among different color or nationality groups in a given period we find that the entire set of political and social forces operating in the period have been responsible. And of these forces discrimination may well be a potent factor. But unemployment differentials by

* Using estimates by the Census survival method for 1870-1950 presented in Everett Lee, et al., *Population Redistribution and Economic Growth in the United States, 1870-1950* (1957), Vol. I, pp. 74-79, 87-90. These data relate to net changes from one Census date to the next, only for native-born. However, the most generous allowance for internal migration of the foreign-born could not bring the sum of these decadal changes up to annual rate since 1947.

** Labor market data from *Manpower Report of the President* (1964), Tables D-6 and D-7. There is reason to believe that these area rates are subject to considerable errors. See J. C. Ullman, "How Accurate Are Estimates of State and Local Unemployment?" *Industrial and Labor Relations Review* (April 1963). It is to be hoped that the biases of estimate are sufficiently random among the areas to permit the generalization we have made in the text.

color or nationality are another matter: in an open society they may well represent way stations as disadvantaged groups shift to areas, occupations, and industries which offer better long-run opportunities. Unemployment is then one of the costs in making such moves: freedom always has its price.

Distressed Areas

Some areas of decline and distress are inevitably left behind in the course of economic change, even in the joyful ascent of the boom and the long swing. This may be a relative decline, as was that of the Carolinas in the 1830's and 1840's when the center of the cotton industry was moving to the Gulf states. It may, however, be an absolute decline. Rochester fell behind in the nineteenth century when wheat milling moved farther west; Lowell, Lawrence, and Paterson fell behind in the twentieth century when the textile industry moved south. Relative declines are inevitable in any economy that opens up new alternatives—through land exploration or technological exploration. These declines become absolute declines of a city or area if no new industries take over and if the forces of decline come with unusual swiftness and comprehensiveness.

In the fall of 1952, some nineteen major U.S. labor market areas were classified as having substantial labor surpluses[22]—and this during a period of intense demand, war production, and wage controls. Brockton, Fall River, Lawrence, Lowell, and New Bedford went into declines as other areas began seizing dominance in textile production and as the demands for other products began receiving far higher priorities than that for textiles. In any economy with effective mobility, however, no substantial number of such areas would be expected to remain in the labor-surplus category very long. Of the sixty-three major labor market areas classified as having a labor surplus in 1958, only three were so classified in 1961—even though 1961 was itself a year of slow growth. This does not, in itself, indicate that there was "enough" mobility; it serves rather to emphasize that at least in the past decade the major distressed areas did not remain permanently in that category.

But in most distributions some extremes can be expected. Table 3 shows the areas classified as having substantial labor surpluses in September of 1955, 1959, and 1963.[23] Pennsylvania clearly stands

out, in its unhappy eminence, having more major and minor depressed labor market areas than any other state over this lengthy
period. West Virginia is a near second (if the fact that it has fewer
reported "labor markets" is taken into account). Kentucky and

Table 3

Areas of Substantial Labor Surplus
(in September 1955, 1959, and 1963)

	Major Areas	Smaller Areas
Pennsylvania	6	15
Massachusetts	4	1
Puerto Rico	2	0
Kentucky	0	3
West Virginia	1	9
45 other states	1	21

Source: U.S. Bureau of Employment Security.

Massachusetts, between them, report more major areas than all
the rest of the states.

Three forces led to this concentration of depressed areas. First,
three of these states, and the depressed areas within them, are
intimately linked to the collapse of coal mining as an industry.
While U.S. employment as a whole was setting new records, an-
thracite coal mining employment plummeted from 75,000 in 1950
to 29,000, and bituminous mining employment from 395,000 to
229,000, by 1957.

But mere decline of industries is not a sufficient explanation.
Other industries had declined nearly as much as coal mining. In
the still shorter period 1953-55, ordnance manufacturing employment fell from 174,000 to 92,000, and railroad employment has
been in a steady decline since 1950 (albeit at a slower rate).[24]
But, barring such concentrations as the railroad shops in Altoona,
these declines have been much more generally dispersed among the
states than was the massive collapse of coal mining.

For unemployment to cumulate in a given area, the decline of
its key industry must be accompanied by the lack of new industries.
Many a city has seen the decline of once proud and dominant
industries but the effects have been offset by the springing up of

new ones. Table 4 shows that the significant growth of employment during the 1950's was particularly associated with the growth of public employment. Hence the extent of growth of public employment might be a significant factor in differentiating the states with distressed-area enclaves from the others. Not enough systematic work has been done on this question to provide a solid basis for inference. But it may not be altogether a coincidence that West Virginia and Kentucky were among the three states in the nation that got the lowest share of military contracts in 1960 relative to their population.[25] And no state with the industrial potential of Pennsylvania received so small a share of contracts in the same year.* Defense production typically involves creating a higher proportion of new products and a higher degree of urgency than is characteristic of civilian production. Technically effective performance carries the banner, and not minimum cost. Growing private industries will seek low costs wherever they appear, and low wage rates associated with depressed areas will be one inducement to entry. But the major growth in the 1950's was in the defense program. Thus fewer contracts were placed in the low-cost depressed areas of the nation than would have been true had there been an equivalent growth of private demand.** Moreover, the growth associated with the construction of local schools and state highways was similarly indifferent to the advantage of low costs in depressed areas.

A third factor in the development of depressed states and regions is the balance of births and mobility. Given two areas with a slow-growing economy, the one with a heavy birth rate and limited outmigration is far more likely to see its unemployment rise than is the one with low birth rates and greater outmigration. This play of forces may be seen in West Virginia and Vermont.

In the period 1920-50, Vermont grew mildly, with no persistently

---

* We measure industrial potential simply as the proportion of all employed persons engaged in nonfarm industry. Data from *1960 Census of Population: U.S. Summary: General Social and Economic Characteristics*, p. 1-281. Pennsylvania, of course, had a greater proportion than states such as Nebraska and Mississippi, which had equally low location quotients but smaller percentages of workers in nonfarm pursuits.

** The second round of procurement, via subcontracts, would have evidenced this differential to a smaller extent. But insofar as cost plus components and urgent completion dates were involved, even this modification might not have been as great as one would anticipate.

Table 4

Labor force and employment change in two postwar decades
(in millions)

	Farming	Manu-facturing	Mining	Con-struction	Transport and utilities	Trade	Finance	Service	Civil govt.	Domestics
Employees										
1919 to 1929	+0.5	0.0	0.0	0.4	-0.1	1.9	0.7	0.5	0.6	0.8
1952 to 1962	+0.1	+0.2	-0.3	0.0	-0.3	1.6	0.7	2.2	2.6	0.7
Difference	-0.4	+0.2	-0.3	-0.4	-0.2	-0.3	0.0	1.7	2.0	-0.1

Labor Force

	Total labor force	Employment		Unemployment
		Public (govt. + A. F.)	Private	
1919 to 1929	+6.8	-0.7	+6.6	+1.0
1952 to 1962	+8.1	+1.8	+4.3	+2.1
Difference	1.3	+2.5	-2.3	+1.1

Sources: (1919-29) in Stanley Lebergott, *Manpower and Economic Growth* (1964), Tables A-3–A-6 (1952-62) *and Manpower Report of the President* (1964), pp. 195, 197, 226.

Note: Estimates of change not additive because of rounding.

rising unemployment and no development of major depressed areas. West Virginia, of course, has accumulated persistent unemployment and major areas of decline. Vermont's population of those aged ten and older grew by about 20 per cent—but because all the growth was taken off in migration, the net population change was almost zero.[26] West Virginia's population, on the other hand, grew by 50 per cent in the face of sharp persistent declines in mining and agricultural activity through much of the period. This rate of increase was equal to California's.[27] It was so great that, despite heavy out-migration, the state's actual population nonetheless rose by 25 per cent. Because its resources and markets did not offer equivalent opportunities, a substantial portion of this increase simply flowed into unemployment and low incomes. When the Malthusian devil combines with the love of home and hearth, one cannot foresee such cumulating unemployment but, retrospectively, one can fairly readily explain it.

Types of Unemployment

We have been discussing the characteristics of the unemployed, but what about the characteristics of unemployment? It is usual to distinguish various types of unemployment—seasonal, frictional, structural, and so on.[28] These distinctions, however, cannot well be applied to the unemployment of any given worker. As Malcolm Denise, Vice-President of Ford, put it:

We have found it impossible to identify any group of laid-off Ford employees whose unemployment is attributable to automation as such. The fact is that changes in processes and technology occur simultaneously with changes in demand, product design, product mix, . . . normal attrition of the work force.[29]

Policy must reckon with the present talents and potential of the unemployed. It is of only limited importance to a physician whether his patient was run over by a Ford or a Chevrolet. It is of limited importance for the re-employment of a given worker whether he lost his job because of automation or because of a decline in demand: what matters overwhelmingly are his abilities for future employment. The past, if relevant at all, is relevant chiefly for whatever help it may give in guessing such abilities.

DO WE HAVE A NEW UNEMPLOYMENT PROBLEM?

Are existing markets becoming saturated? If so our prospects are cloudy indeed. Professor Charles Killingsworth recently told a congressional committee:

. . . our mass consumption society has done a highly effective job of supplying the wants of the great majority of consumers. About 99.5 per cent of the homes that are wired for electricity have electric refrigerators; 93 per cent have television sets. . . . The only sharply rising sales curve in the consumer durables field today is that of the electric can-opener industry.[30]

Now as a general proposition, economists—like businessmen— are wary about arguments that a general saturation of markets is taking place. For example, when Americans achieved a generally adequate diet in the 1920's, they turned their extra productive power (and the income from it) to automobiles. Since World War II, the market for automobiles has continued vigorous but extra incomes have gone at a still greater rate to buy more and better medical care and recreation (through private markets), missiles and schooling (through public channels).

But even though a general saturation is most unlikely, a particular market—or a whole set of them—may indeed wither away. The transition problems thus created by weakening demand can generate a great deal of prolonged unemployment, particularly if sluggish growth is highly concentrated in particular towns and areas.

What can we say about the recent pattern of demand? The path taken by the U.S. economy since World War II has been surveyed from many viewpoints.[31] Table 4 reports the employment changes associated with that pattern of growth and instability and focuses on the most vital employment trends by comparing changes during the 1952-62 decade with those in the longest previous period of peacetime prosperity: the decade 1919-29. Matching employment changes in the two decades, the table shows that the number of employees in farming rose by 0.1 million in 1952-62, or by 0.4 million less than in the earlier period. Smaller gains (or actual declines) were registered in mining, construction, transport, utilities, trade, and domestic service. Finance and manufacturing show almost the same level of advance in both decades.

The slack growth in manufacturing proves to be almost a mirror image of that of the 1920's. Indeed, of all the industry categories only service and government advanced more rapidly in 1952-62 than in 1919-29. There is no need, therefore, to refer to the saturation of consumer needs in an affluent society; nor to a gnawing absence of labor skills requisite for output growth; nor to the impact of trade unions on costs; nor to the rich variety of other "special" factors that have been proposed to explain the experience of the 1950's.*

The table's second section shows that substantially greater gains in the labor force were made in 1952-62. Of these gains, somewhat more than in 1919-29 went into unemployment; far less went into private employment. What shows up most strikingly in 1952-62 is the bounding advance in the public sector. A close look at the gains in that sector indicates that the rises were not in the federal civilian bureaucracy but in the grass-roots govermental units—school districts, cities, states—plus, of course, the armed forces.**

In the aftermath of the war, both consumers and producers plunged into a restocking and investment boom, whose impact was extended to an enormous degree by the Korean War. But by 1957 a turning point had flashed into view.

1. Government expenditures (which had nearly tripled from 1947 to 1952) fell by about 20 per cent from 1952 to 1957.
2. Exports, strong throughout the postwar period, hit their peak in 1957.
3. The cumulation of investment in new production facilities led to a peak of capacity utilization in 1955-56. There followed a decline in 1957, a further decline in 1958, when new facilities came into operation—bringing a levelling off of plant investment.

---

* The pattern for 1952-62 is similar, but shows an even greater weakness in manufacturing.

** Subject to the qualification that the official data do not include figures for the Central Intelligence Agency nor the National Security agencies.

4. Consumer investment in houses and durables peaked in 1955, fell in the generally prosperous year of 1956, showing no further strength in 1957.[32]

The forces behind these peaks were not identical, nor were they intimately linked one with another. (1) The tapering off of government expenditures reflected the 1953 withdrawal from active fighting in Korea. This "shifting of gears" from the acceleration of government expenditures to deceleration created effects on the economy similar to those on passengers when a car that has been swiftly accelerating begins to decelerate. (2) The peaking of exports reflected the maturing of foreign sources of supply after a period of postwar reconstruction. The results were similar to the burgeoning of foreign capacity after World War I, when American agriculture and mining began a similar nosedive. The Marshall Plan, foreign aid, productivity team visits, plus the development of home production in the newly developing countries, all intensified the consequences of the same factors as had appeared in the 1920's. The peaking of plant investment and of consumer investment in durables reflected the inevitable letdown after postwar restocking, after the provision of schools, homes, and facilities linked to the postwar baby boom.

The weaknesses which developed in final sales immediately made their presence known in the labor markets of nearly every industry, occupation, and region. We have a fairly precise view of the performance of the ten major industry groups in the years since 1947:

(A) In the years up to 1956 there had always been one or two groups whose trend was opposite to that of the others in the periods of economic advance. Thus in the six years before 1956 there were fifteen instances of industry unemployment rates running contrary to the national trend. In some years the weakness of particular industries was overcome by the tides of general prosperity. In others, a buoyant rise of employment in particular industries helped moderate a national decline.

(B) In the six years after 1956, however, only three contrary examples appear. This critical shift toward greater conformity took place during a period of slow growth. And its onset suggests that widely pervasive forces were at work, making for general employment declines in response to a general slackening of demand.

24   *Stanley Lebergo*

AUTOMATION—THE DARK SIDE

The thing that scared me to death was Dr. Snyder, who told us tha
computers and automation were destroying jobs at the rate of 40,00
a week. If he is even 10 per cent right we are in trouble.*
—Senator Joseph Clark

The long-run advantage of technological change may be delecta
ble. In the short run such changes may be inevitable. But does eithe
conclusion tell us anything about the problems of the transition
Suppose an economy as dynamic as our own, as Russia's, as Indo
nesia's. Technical advance will occur persistently, continuously. Anc
delight may indeed await everyone in it once the transition is over
But will men thrown out of work find new jobs, adequate ones, by
any given date—or indeed before the day they die? What if the
transition never really is over?

The weakest argument in favor of general joy is that jobs wil
open up in the machine-building industries: by a high irony mer
will find work making the machines that have superseded them
The simplest test of this point is made by checking against our pas
experience. Table 5 shows the count of those employed in producing

Table 5

Employment of wage earners
(in thousands)

1900	29
1929	39
1939	37
1958	37

metal-working machines—including those spectacular machine:
that make other machines:[33]
A half-century of advance had increased employment in this industry
by a mere 10,000 workers.

* Senate Committee on Labor and Public Welfare, *op. cit.*, Part 6, Octobe:
1963, p. 1889. John Snyder, President of U.S. Industries, has stated tha
"automation is eliminating jobs in the United States at the rate of more tha
40,000 a week." "The Ethical Challenge of the Automation Age," in Con
necticut Mutual Life, *Preserving the Individual in an Age of Automatio*
(1963), p. 39.

Suppose that we look at machinery production more generally:[34]

Table 6

Wage earners manufacturing machinery[1]
(in thousands)

	1899	1929	1939	1947	1958
Total	371	748	536	1,244	949
Total except consumer	(350)	(700)	479	1,074	913

[1] Workers employed in the production of refrigerators, sewing machines, and internal combustion engines (mostly for automobiles) are excluded, as such machines superseded few workers.

Employment in *nonconsumer* machinery rose about 12,000 a year from 1899 to 1929; about 80,000 a year from 1939 to 1947. But no gain at all took place from 1947 to 1958—precisely when investment in new equipment reached unprecedented levels. Meanwhile employment in many factory industries dropped: 27,000 jobs were lost annually from 1950-52 to 1960-62 in the primary metal industry alone.* Such a comparison suggests that far more jobs were lost through mechanization than were even remotely created in making the machines for mechanization.

If such pale prospects were all that awaited workers displaced by mechanization, it would be a hardy soul who spoke in favor of it. Constantly rising levels of unemployment, world without end, are hardly acceptable—at least by today's values. But both mechanization and unemployment have been increasing for some time.

Suppose that we compare two historic periods of substantial productivity advance. From 1945 to 1955 output per man-hour jumped 29 per cent—as it had from 1918 to 1929.[35] Equally lively rates of productivity advance occurred in the driving prosperity that followed the end of both world wars. If we apply that implicit rate of job displacement to the beginning-of-period employment totals we would reach the startling conclusion that 12 million jobs were lost in the first decade and 15 million in the second. Yet the actual unemployment percentage rose by only 2.8 points in the first

* For 1952 we exclude June and July, the strike months, since the lower level in those months does not indicate a lower level of jobs but rather of men actually at work.

decade and by only 2.5 points in the second (see Table 7). What
happened was that a combination of lowered prices (resulting from
productivity advance) and increased incomes had generated jobs—
in other industries and in other plants (in many cases, even in
plants that had job losses per unit of product but rises in actual
employment because of increases in units sold).

AUTOMATION—THE GOOD SIDE

The economist's traditional argument for the virtues of technological advance rests on three admirably relevant and quite possibly irresistible considerations.

Destiny. Never argue with an avalanche nor differ with destiny,
says an old Andaman proverb. In most societies, every attempt to
hold back a new system of technology has faltered; nearly every one
has failed. The attractions of the new have proved so overwhelming
to groups not in the happy tradition or monopoly of the old that it
has swept in and replaced the old. The hand-weavers broke the new
power looms—and the hand-weavers disappeared. The flat-glass
blowers passed resolutions and refused to work for companies that
installed the new machines—and the glass-blowers' union died. New
technologies do not spread overnight* (and therein lies the hope of
practical solution), but the multitude of schemes to halt technical
advance in this sector or that, the use of this machine or system or
that, have widely failed. This judgment is, obviously, one not of
moralities or the wisdom of remaining in a technological garden of
Eden—but one of probabilities.

Expediency. Technological advance tends to be linked to some
lively marvelous advantage, private or public. In a private-enterprise
economy, the potential profits to be derived from new techniques
can be so great as to make their introduction irresistibly attractive.
Even if one entrepreneur denies himself such advantage, another is
sure to seize it. Should one firm be prevented by its workers from

---

* Not that delays are not advantageous to particular groups for a time.
English tradition in the 1840's described Jethro Tull as "wicked enough to construct a machine which . . . beat out the corn without manual labour." This
and other new machines were delayed in their introduction. H. J. Habbakuk,
American and British Technology in the Nineteenth Century (1962), pp.
142-43.

Table 7
The Labor Force and Its Components, 1900-60* (in thousands)

Year	Total labor force* Number	Total labor force* Per cent of noninstitutional population	Armed forces	Civilian labor force	Employment Total	Employment Farm	Employment Nonfarm	Unemployment Total	Unemployment Per cent of Civilian labor force	Unemployment Per cent of Nonfarm employees
1900	28,500	55.5	124	28,376	26,956	11,050	15,906	1,420	5.0	12.6
1901	29,268	55.8	115	29,153	27,948	10,916	17,032	1,205	4.0	10.1
1902	30,012	56.0	108	29,904	28,807	10,753	18,054	1,097	3.7	8.6
1903	30,804	56.2	106	30,698	29,494	10,869	18,625	1,204	3.9	9.0
1904	31,548	56.3	107	31,441	29,750	11,076	18,674	1,691	5.4	12.0
1905	32,408	56.5	109	32,299	30,918	11,187	19,731	1,381	4.3	9.5
1906	33,321	56.8	109	33,212	32,638	11,479	21,159	574	1.7	3.9
1907	34,295	57.2	112	34,183	33,238	11,493	21,745	945	2.8	6.0
1908	35,039	57.2	123	34,916	32,136	11,238	20,898	2,780	8.0	16.4
1909	35,855	57.2	134	35,721	33,897	11,163	22,734	1,824	5.1	10.3
1910	36,850	57.4	141	36,709	34,559	11,260	23,299	2,150	5.9	11.6
1911	37,623	57.6	145	37,478	34,960	11,107	23,853	2,518	6.7	13.0
1912	38,081	57.4	149	37,932	36,173	11,136	25,037	1,759	4.6	9.0
1913	38,832	57.3	157	38,675	37,004	10,974	26,030	1,671	4.3	8.2
1914	39,564	57.3	163	39,401	36,281	10,945	25,336	3,120	7.9	14.7
1915	39,774	56.8	174	39,600	36,223	10,953	25,270	3,377	8.5	15.6
1916	40,238	56.6	181	40,057	38,014	10,802	27,212	2,043	5.1	9.1
1917	40,742	56.6	719	40,023	38,175	10,788	27,387	1,848	4.6	8.2
1918	41,980	57.7	2,904	39,076	38,540	10,674	27,866	536	1.4	2.4
1919	41,239	56.4	1,543	39,696	39,150	10,498	28,652	546	1.4	2.4
1920	41,720	55.6	380	41,340	39,208	10,440	28,768	2,132	5.2	8.6
1921	42,341	55.9	362	41,979	37,061	10,443	26,618	4,918	11.7	19.5
1922	42,772	55.7	276	42,496	39,637	10,561	29,076	2,859	6.7	11.4
1923	43,699	55.8	255	43,444	42,395	10,621	31,774	1,049	2.4	4.1
1924	44,502	55.5	267	44,235	42,045	10,599	31,446	2,190	5.0	8.3
1925	45,196	55.4	262	45,169	43,716	10,662	33,054	1,453	3.2	5.4
1926	45,885	55.3	256	45,629	44,828	10,690	34,138	801	1.8	2.9
1927	46,634	55.2	259	46,375	44,856	10,529	34,327	1,519	3.3	5.4
1928	47,367	55.2	262	47,105	45,123	10,497	34,626	1,982	4.2	6.9
1929	48,017	55.1	260	47,757	46,207	10,541	35,666	1,550	3.2	5.3
1930	48,783	55.0	260	48,523	44,183	10,340	33,843	4,340	8.9	14.2
1931	49,585	55.2	260	49,325	41,305	10,240	31,065	8,020	16.3	25.2
1932	50,348	55.4	250	50,098	38,038	10,120	27,918	12,060	24.1	36.3
1933	51,132	55.6	250	50,882	38,052	10,090	27,962	12,830	25.2	37.6
1934	51,910	55.7	260	51,650	40,310	9,990	30,320	11,340	22.0	32.6
1935	52,553	55.6	270	52,283	41,673	10,110	31,563	10,610	20.3	30.2
1936	53,319	55.7	300	53,019	43,989	10,090	33,899	9,030	17.0	25.4
1937	54,088	55.9	320	53,768	46,068	10,000	36,068	7,700	14.3	21.3
1938	54,872	56.0	340	54,532	44,142	9,840	34,302	10,390	19.1	27.9
1939	55,588	56.0	370	55,218	45,738	9,710	36,028	9,480	17.2	25.2
1940	56,180	56.0	540	55,640	47,520	9,540	37,980	8,120	14.6	21.3
1941	57,530	56.7	1,620	55,910	50,350	9,100	41,250	5,560	9.9	14.4
1942	60,380	58.8	3,970	56,410	53,750	9,250	44,500	2,660	4.7	6.8
1943	64,560	62.3	9,020	55,540	54,470	9,080	45,390	1,070	1.9	2.7
1944	66,040	63.1	11,410	54,630	53,960	8,950	45,010	670	1.2	1.7
1945	65,290	61.9	11,430	53,860	52,820	8,580	44,240	1,040	1.9	2.7
1946	60,970	57.2	3,450	57,520	55,250	8,320	46,930	2,270	3.9	5.5
1947	61,758	57.4	1,590	60,168	57,812	8,256	49,557	2,356	3.9	5.4
1948	62,898	57.9	1,456	61,442	59,117	7,960	51,156	2,325	3.8	5.1
1949	63,721	58.0	1,616	62,105	58,423	8,017	50,406	3,682	5.9	8.0
1950	64,749	58.4	1,650	63,099	59,748	7,497	52,251	3,351	5.3	7.1
1951	65,983	58.9	3,097	62,884	60,784	7,048	53,736	2,099	3.3	4.4
1952	66,560	58.8	3,594	62,966	61,035	6,792	54,243	1,932	3.1	4.0
1953	67,362	58.5	3,547	63,815	61,945	6,555	55,390	1,870	2.9	3.8
1954	67,818	58.4	3,350	64,468	60,890	6,495	54,395	3,578	5.6	7.1
1955	68,896	58.7	3,048	65,848	62,944	6,718	56,225	2,904	4.4	5.7
1956	70,387	59.3	2,857	67,530	64,708	6,572	58,135	2,822	4.2	5.4
1957	70,744	58.7	2,797	67,946	65,011	6,222	58,789	2,936	4.3	5.6
1958	71,284	58.5	2,637	68,647	63,966	5,844	58,122	4,681	6.8	8.7
1959	71,946	58.3	2,552	69,394	65,581	5,836	59,745	3,813	5.5	7.0
1960	73,126	58.3	2,514	70,612	66,681	5,723	60,958	3,931	5.6	7.1

* Age 14 and over.
Source: Stanley Lebergott, *Manpower in Economic Growth* (1961), Appendix Table A-3.

adopting a novel production technique, another firm is likely to b
out of reach of such constraints. (Its workers may be more feebl
organized; its management may be fighting for survival, or wholl
confident in its rights.)

In a world of aggressively independent nation states, the natio
seizing upon a more efficient technology becomes able to produc
more cheaply, to sell at a lower price. It can happily invade the e
port markets of nations that deny themselves such technological ac
vantage. This consideration is as compelling to a socialist state as t
a venture capital nation. For instance, American coal has bee
mined in a highly unionized industry from veins of dwindling ricl
ness and shipped in vessels with transportation costs among th
highest in the world. Yet it could compete in Newcastle, invad
Polish markets, and sell in many another country—all for one reason
American coal companies and labor unions have cooperated in ir
troducing the most complex and unbelievable of new machines an
new production techniques to this elderly industry. The prudent an
religious attachment of European miners to traditional technique
could not hold back the buyers, whose interest was in cheap coa
and not in coal that had been produced with a "personal touch."

Social Advantage. Whatever the shape of a society, its membe
will (other things being equal) generally prefer more goods to les
This will surely be true if the mass of the people lack food fron
time to time (or lack enough food at all times), or if their childre
fail to get proper medical attention, decent schooling, and adequat
housing. The feebler the productivity of a society, the more certai
it is that its members will be condemned to live in such want. Bt
the more that the productivity of a society advances, the more goo
it can produce with the same complement of resources—howeve
sterile the land or scanty the mineral deposits—and the greater th
chance of an advance in the goods and services available to th
mass of the people. And it is the introduction of new technologie
that make possible just such critical advance.

It is mere "nonsense on stilts" to argue that the increase in produ
tion potential is not vital—is not, indeed, the job of an econom
Few people expound the advantages of wealth: it is the virtues an
rewards of poverty that are expounded by moralists and others, a
though the common experience of mankind proves poverty asso
ciated with misery, want, and premature death.

The adoption of new technologies has been so common over the centuries despite man's desire for stability because these new technologies make possible a greater output—not at the price of more arduous work and longer hours but, typically, with easier work and shorter hours. Whether this potential is used to bring about a more equitable distribution of a society's goods among its members and to provide for the well-being of those displaced by the new technologies is a problem which must be solved by the political and economic order. But it is a problem infinitely preferable to that presented by an inadequate supply of goods fought over by the starving members of a stagnant society. In sum, the triple combination of destiny, expediency, and social advantage constitutes the hard basis on which technological advance has been, and will continue to be, justified.

TECHNOLOGICAL CHANGE AND SKILL DEMANDS

Forecasts that over the next decade bounding increases will take place in the requirements for skill turn on a variety of assumptions. The issues are far too complex to settle here, but we may at least note three of the central considerations involved.

At its simplest level, the prediction of rising skill requirements is an extrapolation of the rising level of education that marks the United States labor force. In 1940, the typical male worker had 8.7 years of schooling; in 1952, 10.4 years; in 1962, 12.1 years.[36] The figures, however, do not indicate whether higher educational requirements were set by employers or whether increasing amounts of schooling were administered to the young so that they all simply entered the labor force with more schooling. The census reports show, for example, a rise between 1940 and 1962 of 1.2 years in the schooling of the typical laborer, and a rise between 1952 and 1962 of 1.1 years in the schooling of farm laborers and of 0.6 years in the schooling of female domestics. Should we conclude that the formal education requirements for domestic service rose, or those for common labor were extended? Or should we reserve judgment on the possibility that the shift of population to urban areas and the expansion of facilities for public education simply endowed the average worker with longer schooling—and not necessarily in response to labor market demands?

A more potent argument for predictions of increases in skill requirements points to the growth of those industries that typically require their workers to pass through extended periods of schooling. The boldest rise in employment from 1950 to 1960 took place in the government and service sectors. Both are major employers of high school and college graduates. Of the 1.4 million increase in the number of professional and kindred workers over this decade, we must attribute about 0.8 million to the demands for teachers, about 0.2 million to the demand for medical personnel, and most of the rest to the vast increase of engineers, draftsmen, scientists, and the like, in the defense program.[37]

Forecasts of a continued increase in requirements for professionally trained workers therefore tend to be implicit predictions of continued employment growth in government. What are the present employment prospects in the areas—teaching, national defense, and medical care—noted above? Suppose a continued lively increase in the demand for teachers may reasonably be anticipated. Is such a demand more likely to be met by training the typical member of the labor force to new educational heights or by attracting women away from home pursuits and from less-skilled work? Defense employment requirements will undoubtedly increase. But the frame of reference here should be the doubling (in real terms) of defense spending that took place from 1950 to 1960. Matched against that standard, what about the modest rises in defense expenditures since 1954 and the cresting of such expenditures scheduled for the near future? Can we forecast from these a rise in the demand for professionals in any way comparable to that generated by the intensive defense program of 1950-60? *

Consider, instead of the relatively small college group the much larger group of those with high school training. The persistent rise in the demand for high school graduates (as clerks and minor functionaries in banks, insurance companies, factory offices, and brokerage houses) has been a blatant fact of the postwar era. But if the computer revolution foreseen as a spur to the demand for more

---

* A rising hypochondria level may well warrant projecting more medical care employment, as would further income rises. However some blunting of these projections to allow for perhaps a once-for-all gain in personnel resulting from the initial spread of Blue Cross and Blue Shield may be worth considering.

educated workers is real, it will become real by substituting machines for men and women in just such activities. Computers are outrageously competent, swift, and accurate in performing the clerical tasks to be found in stores, banks, factory offices, insurance companies. And if these computers, together with other machines, are introduced at the rate predicted, they will perform their functions at the expense of the clerks and salesmen who are high school graduates, rather than at the expense of the janitors or domestic servants who have only been through grade school.

The most dramatic impact of the automation revolution, however, is expected to be the reshaping of factory production lines. It is here that the decline in the demand for unskilled labor and the further rise in the demand for superior skills (to meet the new machine technology) are predicted as certain. How is our past experience to be evaluated? It is, of course, absurdly easy to find examples of transitions in production techniques that did increase or decrease requirements for skill and education. But what, on balance, has occurred? No satisfactory answer can yet be given on this critical issue: We simply do not have a broad enough basis of knowledge. As a rough second-best, we may look at two pieces of evidence.

The first is what appears to be the most extensive study yet made of the process of automation: a survey, conducted by James Bright, of thirteen plants employing almost 50,000 persons.[38] Bright finds that the introduction of automated procedures in these plants required no extensive retraining of the existing labor force. Nor did it lead to the development of any marked increase in skill requirements. The automated production systems in the plants studied "involved about 5000 persons and were serviced by 2000 to 3000 maintenance men," but "less than a dozen instances were encountered where an operation required new calibers of direct or indirect labor skills. . . . In fact automation often tends to reduce the skill and training required of the work force."

The proposition that experience since the 1956 peak has reflected something flashier than the mere dull downturn of the business cycle—some twist peculiar to the operation of the labor market—can be tested in another way.

Consider the relationship between the percentage of manufacturing employees who are unemployed and the percentage of

manufacturing capital (i.e., plant and equipment) that is lying idle.*
The two percentages ought to move together in corresponding patterns over the typical business cycle. And in fact—for the period
1949-55—they do. (The correlation between them, if perfect, would
be 1.00; the 1949-55 figure is close: 0.89.) Now suppose that for some
technicality in the labor market workers became displaced and/or
unemployable at an increasing rate after 1955. We should then expect this relationship between the two percentages to change
sharply. If, for example, a great amount of investment in automated
equipment had been made, the new equipment would surely be
utilized much more fully than the old equipment had been. Designed to be operated by fewer workers (or none at all), it
could normally be used on two or even three shifts a day, whereas
older equipment, linked to men, would have been used on only one
or at most two shifts a day. Moreover new equipment would also
tend to be used rather fully as compared to the antiquated equipment that it had retired from use. On the other hand, just the opposite situation would prevail in the employment of men. The
proportion of unemployed workers would grow. Dismissed because
of their outmoded skills (or lack of skills), most of the men would
linger in the labor force, vainly seeking work.

These forces would jointly tend to create a growing proportion of
capital in use, and a declining proportion of labor employed. Hence
we would look for a marked change in the relationship between the
two unemployment rates after the date when automation speeded
up. The correlation should fall, and probably fall very significantly
if this hypothesis of massive displacement picture were valid.

But the facts do not confirm it. The correlation for the 1949-55
period is 0.89, and for 1956-63 it is 0.90—almost unchanged.** Of

* For this computation we use unpublished data on the proportion of wage
and salary workers in manufacturing that were unemployed (seasonally adjusted) and data on manufacturing output as a percent of capacity. These
data were kindly provided by Robert Stein of the U.S. Bureau of Labor Statistics and Frank de Leeuw of the Federal Reserve Board.

** The constant, in the linear regression used, fell from 0.9 to −0.4.
The coefficient for time (in quarters) was 0.02 in the later period. Hence,
e.g., the rise in worker unemployment from a 4.4 to a 9.5 rate between the
first quarter of 1956 and that of 1961 would be overwhelmingly explained
by the rise in excess plant. The equation would forecast a rise of 4.6 per cent
because of plant plus 0.03 per cent because of factors associated with time—
giving 9.26 compared to the actual 9.5.
For 1956-63, measuring the worker unemployment rate as UL, that of

the increase in labor unemployment over these two periods, well over 90 per cent is accounted for by the same forces that are linked to the rise in excess plant unemployment. The trend factors (of which, of course, only a part is linked to automation) account for only a trivial portion of the rise.

To what does all this lead? Primarily to this conclusion: we cannot forecast confidently that constantly rising levels of education and skill will be demanded by the production techniques of the future. There is, of course, every likelihood that our polity and society will give the generations ahead more and more formal schooling. And because in that future, as now, business firms must choose their employees from the existing labor force, they will therefore be hiring workers who are better educated. But that such firms will require a sharply rising level of education and skill is another matter. To the extent that projections of such requirements turn on an extrapolation of the recent past they extrapolate trends in defense spending, in postwar birth rates, and other factors to a degree that may well be dramatically excessive. To the extent they forecast the increasing substitution of skilled for unskilled labor as a result of automation they ignore the conflicting evidence on whether such trends are taking place even now. More important, they ignore the possibility that machines may be substituted for the better-educated workers as well. Hence the displacement of the relatively low-skilled workers as a result of a massive increase in employer demands for higher skills is by no means certain—and does not warrant forecasts of sharp rises in unemployment.

STRUCTURAL PROBLEMS OR FEEBLE DEMAND?

Why has the rising level of unemployment since 1957 generated so much—and such increasing—concern? Over 12 million workers became unemployed during 1951—the peak of the war-production prosperity.* Yet it can hardly be said that unemployment was one of

---

capital as UK, and time (in quarters) as T, the equation used is: $UL = -0.48 + 0.36\ UK + 0.02T$. $R = 0.90$; $R^{-2} = 0.812$.

* U.S. Bureau of the Census, *Annual Report on the Labor Force, 1951*, Table 20. This figure is the sum of gross additions to unemployment. Since the same worker could become unemployed more than once during the year, the number should be matched not against the total labor force but to the labor force plus the sum of additions to the labor force during the year—or roughly 100 million.

the significant economic issues of that year. Why not? The answer probably lies in the fact that the long-duration unemployed averaged about 0.5 million—or not even 1 per cent of the total labor force. The most serious human aspects of unemployment are not those linked to total unemployment; they are confined to the hard-core, long-duration, unemployed—defined roughly as those who have been without work for fifteen weeks or more. An economy can tolerate a certain level of unemployment, as an individual puts up with a minor case of flu or a broken toe. But hard-core unemployment reflects something more serious than unemployment per se. As such it demands active and perhaps extensive intervention to reduce it. It is this difference between the total number of unemployed and the hard-core unemployed that distinguishes what the U.S. has come to consider a politically live issue.

The hard-core unemployed averaged about 0.5 million a year from 1947 right through 1957 (see Table 8). In 1958 it rose abruptly to about 1.5 millions, and has continued at double or triple the 1947-57 levels every year since.

One explanation of this increase has been offered by those who contend that automation is eliminating about 2 million jobs a year in the United States. Now it is clear that in the century and a half of our national life there has been no time when workers were not being displaced by ever more efficient machinery. In 1815, for example, 100 operatives were required to run 1000 cotton spindles; by 1860, 77 of those operatives were superfluous.[39] The classic discussion of changing manpower requirements in the dynamic manufacturing sector concludes that of 100 wage earners required per unit of output in 1899, 53 were no longer needed in 1939.[40]

Hence, the rise of hard-core unemployment from modest proportions in 1947-57 to a much higher level since 1958 cannot be explained simply on the basis of productivity advance, for this force has been operating throughout the nation's recorded history. Nor can it be explained by changes in the techniques of productivity advance. The critical point is: Did jobs begin to disappear at a faster rate after 1957? (And, as a check, another question: Has the unemployment resulting from productivity gains begun to cumulate at a faster rate in recent years?)

In answering these questions, it will be most useful to examine the record of the manufacturing sector, for it is this sector that typically

Table 8

Unemployed persons, by duration of unemployment, 1947-63
(in thousands of persons 14 years of age and over)

		Duration of unemployment			
	Total unemployed	4 weeks and under	5-14 weeks	15-26 weeks	Over 26 weeks
1947	2,356	1,255	704	234	164
1948	2,325	1,349	669	193	116
1949	3,682	1,804	1,195	427	256
1950	3,351	1,515	1,055	425	357
1951	2,099	1,223	574	166	137
1952	1,932	1,183	517	148	84
1953	1,870	1,178	482	132	79
1954	3,578	1,651	1,115	495	317
1955	2,904	1,387	815	367	336
1956	2,822	1,485	805	301	232
1957	2,936	1,485	890	321	239
1958	4,681	1,833	1,397	785	667
1959	3,813	1,658	1,113	469	571
1960	3,931	1,798	1,176	502	454
1961	4,806	1,897	1,375	728	804
1962	4,007	1,754	1,134	534	585
1963	4,166	1,847	1,231	535	553

Source: Manpower Report of the President, 1964.

paces the economy in both upturns and declines and demonstrates almost daily the most spectacular effects of automation. In Table 8, the U.S. Bureau of Labor Statistics estimates of the number of factory workers and the rate of change in manpower requirements per unit of factory output provide an indication of the economy's performance: *

* Data from the Manpower Report of the President, 1964, pp. 163, 199. We estimate job changes associated with productivity advance by assuming that the reported changes in output per man-hour 1947-57 could be applied beginning with the 1947 employment figure, and the 1957-62 change beginning with the 1957 employment total. The difference between such changes, with a constant demand, and the actual change, reflects the net of the demand changes.

Table 9

Job changes in manufacturing (annual average)
(in thousands)

| | Associated with | | Actual employment change |
	Productivity advance	Demand increases	
1947-57	−540	+560	+20
1957-62	−584	+308	−276

The figures do indicate a substantial loss of jobs, in both periods
as a result of productivity advances. But was the rate of loss greate
in the more recent period, when automation was presumably havin;
its sharpest effects in generating unemployment? The answer pro
vided by this dynamic sector, where the most flamboyant automa
tion advances have taken place, is a clear "No." Only the sharp shif
in demand can explain the significant rise in actual factory employ
ment in 1947-57 and the substantial fall in 1957-62.

To this point we have looked merely at the figures on job loss. Bu
job loss is not identical with unemployment. Suppose (unreal
istically) that productivity advances only in factories with boomin;
sales. Then the job losses would be wholly hypothetical: fewer mei
would be required to accommodate the higher output, but not
single man would actually be thrown out of work.

Special studies by the Bureau of Labor Statistics make it possibl
to get a better sight on the actual extent of worker displacement.[4]
These studies report that manufacturing workers were displaced a
a rate of about 90,000 a year in 1947-57 and 170,000 a year in 1957
62. The increase of 100,000 a year by no means accounts for ou
experience since 1957, but it was an important complement to th
demand weakness indicated in Table 8.

There is perhaps no need to ride the obvious meaning of suc
productivity displacements. They occur as part of the process o
cutting production costs and introducing new products. Thus the
sustain the job market for those who remain employed in th
factories affected. Had productivity advance been more hesitant i
recent years, production costs would have risen still more, inducin

more imports, a shift to other expenditure items and, thereby, a still deeper decline of factory employment.*

SOLUTIONS

Unemployment is an almost inevitable characteristic of a free labor market, in which workers may quit their jobs and employers may fire their workers without government interference. (With the relaxation of government control over their labor markets, the Soviet Union and Poland have also experienced a growth of unemployment.) But the impact of unemployment on both the individual and the society is potentially so devastating that solutions for this problem are constantly proposed. Before looking at some of the more recent proposals we must recognize three points.

First, society always pays a price for unemployment. "The Fourteenth Amendment did not enact Mr. Herbert Spencer's *Social Statics*," Justice Holmes once protested. But even in the days when it looked as though it had, employers with high layoff rates were being penalized.

For so long as workers prefer stable employment to irregular, short-term employment, wage differentials will tend to reflect this preference. Farmers have typically had to pay higher rates to laborers hired by the day than to those hired by the month. Masons, confronted by more irregular work prospects than carpenters because of the weather, have usually commanded higher rates of pay.[42] And in the 1960's, the rising probability of technological unemployment tomorrow has raised wage rates and labor costs today. Where rates have not changed, fringe benefits have been increased —most noticeably in the form of automation funds. (Such adjustments may, nonetheless, fall far short of what society might wish to do for the unemployed. Indeed, the major comprehensive study of these funds concludes that they "provide little or nothing in the way of benefits for the workers displaced by automation"—focusing, rather, on maintaining the incomes of retained workers.[43]

---

* Where monopolies or other tightly controlled markets are involved, of course, no such inference is warranted. But a look at the major areas of technological advance does not suggest that such qualifications are important in the present context.

Second, the decade of the 1930's provided some harsh lessons in economic stability. Just what these were is hardly a matter of gospel. Here we take in evidence two major congressional actions. The first is the establishment of the unemployment insurance system and its corollary, experience rating. The second is the passage of the Employment Act of 1946 (and its corollary Congressional and Administration actions in the recessions of 1948-49, 1953-54, 1957-58, and 1960-61). The first act assumes that it is salutary to penalize the consumer, through the employer, for unemployment created in the process of producing what he will buy; the second, that the private market cannot be counted upon to generate, by itself, charges against incomes in a way that will prevent the rise of unemployment to critical levels.

Third, the nation's economy, beginning in 1940, was so reorganized, pushed, and adjusted as to create a greater peacetime stability (if stability is measured in one relevant sense: namely, the rise and fall of unemployment). Since 1900 the United States has had three periods of prolonged peacetime prosperity: 1900-17, 1920-29, and 1947-63. In the first period the unemployment rate changed by less than two percentage points a year in ten of the seventeen years (and by more, in seven). In the second period the rate changed by less than 2 per cent in three years (and by more, in six). But from 1947 to 1963 changes under 2 per cent were overwhelmingly typical: fourteen years out of the sixteen. Hence despite the volatile course of federal expenditures (and perhaps, in part, because of it), the fluctuation of unemployment was much more restrained in 1947-63 than in the two earlier periods of prosperity. The cycle is still there: it has not been tamed. But it has been distinctly less voracious. The underemployment equilibrium of the early 1960's appears to differ significantly from that of the early 1930's.

Unemployment levels since 1957 have been low, as compared with most prewar standards. Yet neither national party nor any Administration has treated the rise as insignificant or commended the unemployed to local charity and civic action. Opinions do clash, however, as to the underlying causes of the unemployment and, hence, as to what constitutes appropriate federal action.

One school of thought emphasizes the differences among the unemployment rates of various groups (e.g., whites and nonwhites) and changes in such relationships between prosperity and depression.[44] According to Congressman MacGregor of Minnesota:

. . . when we note the composition of the prosperity unemployed as being primarily the unskilled workers, we come to the conclusion that retraining on both a short- and long-term basis is one of the most potent suggestions for improving employment opportunities.[45]

Congressman Curtis of Missouri concluded that the Council of Economic Advisers has approached the problem of employment

by riveting its attention on aggregate unemployment, . . . suggesting that our economy has not been attaining its economic potential, while people like myself believe the problem is primarily one of unfilled employment opportunities resulting from unusually rapid economic growth. We concentrate our attention for further growth on filling these employment opportunities. . . . This analysis leads us to establish programs to make workers skilled and to keep federal monetary and fiscal policies neutral.[46]

Perhaps the most succinct summary of this approach is a magazine article reporting that unemployment today is "skilled jobs begging for men and unskilled men begging for jobs." In a study of eleven areas, the authors found that

. . . industry would take more skilled men . . . if it could find them. If you argue that some workers left [unemployed] . . . are skilled workers, you will meet the counterargument that they are too old. The old, according to industry, cease to be skilled when they slow down to a certain point.

The interesting thing about this article is that it appeared in 1937, when there were about 9 million unemployed.[47] If critical observers could be struck by vacancies waiting for skilled workers in 1937, it is hardly surprising that they should note such vacancies in 1964. (Neither observation, of course, tells us that the substance of the current problem is not inadequate demand but a lack of skills in some absolute sense.)

The emphasis on the need for more education and skill—in which reactions to Sputnik combined with concern over the unemployment

problem and the rise in high school and college registration—led to
the Manpower Development and Training Act of 1962.* It is not
that Congress had ignored vocational training before that, but the
courses established by the various states—with federal help—were
singularly removed from the current problem. The new Act wisely
required that training be restricted to those occupations in which
there was some reasonable prospect of employment. (Of those boys
receiving full-time training under the older, state programs in 1962,
474,118—or two thirds—were being trained in agriculture, a field in
which employment has been declining ever since 1910.[48])

The retraining approach that Congress adopted with singular
unanimity must, however, be viewed primarily as a solution for the
long-run problems of labor market reallocation; it is not a solution
for the immediate problems of unemployment for two reasons:

(1) The proposals are limited in scope. It would take forty
years to eliminate present unemployment through retraining, given
fiscal 1964 costs and appropriations—even if no more workers ever
became unemployed. Given the novelty of the program, and the
hesitancy with which the states have gone ahead on contributing
their financial share, it is not surprising that Congress should have
limited the program. In consequence, the most arduous and un-
ceasing efforts of those involved have been required to train fewer
people each year—on thousands of different projects in the fifty
states and territories—than are trained in one year by one major
corporation.** The target set by Congress of approximately 130,000
workers retrained each year for three years, compared with the
more than 4 million unemployed in the spring of 1964, indicates the
magnitude of the problem.[49]

(2) By April 1963, some 234,000 candidates for the manpower
retraining program had been given screening interviews by the U.S.
Employment Service;—of whom less than 10 per cent were referred
for training.[50] Of the 10 per cent chosen, two thirds were in the
prime twenty-two–forty-four age group and half had been unemployed for less than fifteen weeks. Yet about one third of this

---

* The Act, as amended in 1964, is well worth reading as an indication of
Congressional thought and intent.
** Arnold R. Weber, *Retraining the Unemployed*, reports that IBM trains
100,000 persons annually in computer operation "to provide the personnel
needed to man the machines it sells and leases" and reports a *Fortune* estimate that GM retrains about 7,200 of its workers annually for complex jobs.

highly select group did not find work after they had been retrained.*

Now if only two thirds of the best 10 per cent of the unemployed screened for training actually found work, it is abundantly clear that retraining is not the answer to the aggregate unemployment problems of the early 1960's. (Had the administrators been so unwise as to choose for retraining not the most employable but the lame, the halt, and the aged, the re-employment rate would have been even lower, and public criticism enormous.) It is important to note that by any realistic standards the re-employment rate is high. This new program placed 70 per cent of its trainees, an employment rate almost equal to that of young workers coming out of traditional vocational courses. (Sweden's long-established programs placed only about 75 per cent.[51])

Present training programs must be treated primarily as attempts to pioneer in the difficult task of reorienting workers whose long-term prospects are otherwise for low incomes and irregular employment. The gains to the individual are high (for the young trainee they are estimated at better than $50,000 over his work life); the gains to the government (in terms of reduced relief spending and increased tax revenues) are clearly likely to repay the average cost of $1,200 to $1,500 per worker many times over. But "more important than all these calculations is the fact that we would halt the deterioration process not only for the individuals involved, but for their children and succeeding generations."[52] Under the circumstances, the merits of the program are in no way qualified by the conclusion—at existing financial and selectivity levels—that it provides no solution whatever to the nation's unemployment problem.

AN UNEMPLOYMENT TARGET

How much unemployment must capitalism have to continue functioning? How many workers must be jobless for any free economy simply to operate? And how much unemployment is consistent with

* The one-third ratio applies only to those completing training. (Of the 5,141 enrolled, only 4,009 completed training, the others being forced back into the job market by financial need or inability. The recent amendments to the Act should, by extending financial help, minimize such loss.) By the end of 1963, the re-employment rate was much the same: 70.1 per cent. See *Report of the Secretary of Labor on Manpower Research and Retraining* (March 1964), p. 33.

price stability? Such questions, asked by friend and foe alike, typically lie behind attempts to determine a frictional minimum of unemployment as a guide to government policy.

Perhaps the most relevant answer to such questions is this: capitalism does not require *any* unemployment to operate efficiently. Free-market economies have *no* technical requirements that make unemployment necessary. True, some employers agree with Marx that an industrial reserve army of the unemployed is a superb device for keeping labor docile and cheap. And some workers are living examples of Young's wide-ranging assertion: "Everyone knows that the unemployed are victims of their own idle and irregular courses." But whether a capitalist system requires unemployment is quite another matter.

The assumption that it must springs from a belief that economic advance produces unemployment:

Every new fashion, every new machine . . . has a tendency to render more useful the service of one class of artisans and less useful those of another . . . the natural remedy is that the workmen . . . should betake themselves to the new sources of employment which almost always accompany, and generally have, in fact, occasioned the change. . . . [But] they dislike change, and particularly a change by which a portion of their skill becomes useless, and they may have to act under a new master, with new associates, and often in a new residence. Nothing but necessity, therefore, will impel them to a change of occupations." [53]

So wrote Senior in 1841. For *necessity* read *unemployment* and you have today's problem.

We too know the combination of growth and decline. Silk and rayon textiles falter as nylon becomes popular. Cabriolets disappear, and Model T's, then coupe de ville's, take their place. Texas oil now fuels an economy that once burned brightly with coal from West Virginia and Pennsylvania.

Such shifts do of course demand reallocation of labor, capital, and materials. But is resource flexibility the same thing as unemployment? Discussions of the reallocation of capital do not focus on its shifts from unemployment (i.e., cash), but on its key shifts from lower- to higher-yielding investments.[54] Similarly, it is the total pattern by which labor is reallocated from one use to another that should be examined, not merely the portion that becomes unemployed in the process.

Such an examination will show that the American labor market offers substantial possibilities for reallocation by procedures other than unemployment. In 1961 unemployment averaged 4,806,000. In the same year:[55]

4,480,000 persons changed jobs without becoming unemployed (and because they did so more than once, they filled an average of 7,260,000 jobs);

3 million persons held second jobs in addition to their primary jobs;

3 million other persons were partially unemployed during the year (put on short work weeks by their employers because sales were low, and so on) who normally worked a full year.[56]

Note that in a recession year—and such years are never notable for resource flexibility—about as many people changed jobs without becoming unemployed as were unemployed. And considerably more persons had second jobs or worked a short week (thus permitting their employers to extend or cut down on the volume of their production without actually creating unemployment). But such shifts from job to job and shifts in response to varying production needs are precisely the reasons why it is usually argued that unemployment is required for the functioning of an economy. Here we have a clear demonstration of still greater adjustments through the labor market than in fact take place through unemployment.

The ground on which all this rests is the considerable drive and ingenuity American workers display in finding work and in making whatever shifts are needed to improve their lot. Most American workers regard job shifts as quite natural—unlike workers in some other countries, whose goal is to remain on a given payroll for life. A comprehensive survey by the Census Bureau in the prosperity year of 1951 showed that men aged twenty to twenty-four had spent 1.2 years on their present jobs; men aged thirty-five to forty-four, 4.5 years; and men aged fifty-five to sixty-four, 9.3 years. Note that men in the older age group, though in the labor force for nearly forty years, had been at their present jobs for less than ten of those years.[57]

The average man enters the labor force at nineteen and quits at sixty-two.[58] Since he spends about four years on a given job (according to the Census survey) he will have had about eleven different jobs in his work lifetime.[59]

If most of the reallocation of labor in the economy does not take place through unemployment but, rather, by direct shifts job to job, by changes from full-time to part-time employment and back again, by entrances into and withdrawals from the labor force, what is the point of going on to assert that a capitalist economy doesn't require any unemployment to function effectively? First, to help distinguish the goal (efficient resource allocation) from one means (unemployment). Second, to emphasize the fact that there may be a choice among various means—and it is here that the field for policy choices widens.

A Political-Social Minimum

A capitalist economy does not require that even one of its workers ever be unemployed. But a democratic, open social order surely does. The reason? Simply that a central goal of such an order is freedom of choice. It is always possible to remove unemployment by denying such choice—using the threat of legal action, rigorous custom, or starvation to force people to work. Most Western nations have chosen instead to develop social insurance systems. One central purpose of such systems is to prolong unemployment, to make it sufficiently bearable so that men need not be forced to take the first job available regardless of pay or working conditions. They have extended this option to sustain purchasing power and production, to minimize those discontents that menace the social order itself, and to assure a social order in which men are more likely to take risks, to move on to new jobs, to share in those resource shifts that are essential for a society's growth.

Freedom of choice is exercised in the choice by employer and worker. The employer has freedom to hire and to fire. Of course, he encounters penalties in the form of charges for unemployment insurance (through experience rating), dismissal wage costs, and the reactions of employees and trade unions. But the briefest look at the sizable volume of firings (workers left about 4 million jobs in 1961 because of layoffs) demonstrates that the employer's prerogatives are not merely hypothetical.[60]

Most free-market economies do not require an employer to hire any given worker or a worker to take any given job. It is a natural corollary that an employer may reject a job applicant and an employee may reject a job offer in order to look for something better—however unrealistic such a search may appear to an omniscient observer.

How can these conflicting goals, interests, and opinions be combined into a minimum unemployment goal for consideration by Congress and the Administration, both of which persistently give evidence of trying to keep unemployment down to "acceptable" levels.

One possible criterion, recently suggested by the Commission on Money and Credit, is to aim for something like a 1:1 ratio of unfilled job vacancies to unemployment.[61] Such measures are perhaps worth investigation, but they are likely to be of limited practical consequence because they are likely to affect only slightly the factors that determine major monetary and fiscal choices. Suppose, for example, that unemployment rises to 10 million persons. A major issue will confront the nation, regardless of what a job-vacancy total or ratio may show. In the end it is the unemployment rate that will determine the seriousness of the unemployment situation as judged by most Americans, and by the govermental authorities as well. If job-vacancy data confirm the rate, they will be supererogatory; if they conflict with what employment data tell us, they will be cast aside.*

A Frictional Minimum

Responsible Congressmen, Board members of the Federal Reserve Banks throughout the nation, the Administration—all must deal

---

* A vacancy for one exotic dancer will not cancel out the unemployment of one auto worker, and a job in California will not cancel out an unemployed worker in West Virginia. Hence it will be necessary to assess the commutability of vacancies and unemployed. Unless this leads to a proliferation of ratios it will probably lead to a short hand tactic of referring to the ratio or gap in a period of time that we consider generally suitable. Unless this reference were to be a casual affair it would require experience over at least one business cycle before one could effectively use such data.

with the unemployment problem. They may adopt new measures, accelerate old ones, prevent action on those they believe to be unwise.

What is a practicable unemployment goal for them? The answer will depend on the way in which the question is defined: How can we have minimum price gains consistent with, e.g., 3 per cent unemployment? Or: How can we have minimum unemployment consistent with price stability (i.e., 0 per cent inflation)? Both are intelligible goals. Neither can be achieved without a cost in alternatives. When society considers unemployment as evidence of sin, incompetence, or merely an unfortunate but inevitable aspect of economic activity, it may take little collective action. When it begins to consider unemployment as evidence of an individual or societal malfunction, requiring remedy, it will do more. The present period is one in which these values are shifting.

In the depression of the 1930's, as unemployment kept increasing to its peak level in 1932 (when 24 per cent of the labor force was jobless), the advisers to the President considered the problem urgent, but not serious—at least not serious enough for the federal government to assume "the major role," and thereby threaten "the whole foundations of local government, which is the very basis of self-government." [62]

Since that time the entire nation has changed its way of thinking. It is hardly likely that any contemporary President in the midst of a major recession would declare that "As a nation we must prevent hunger and cold to those of our people who are in honest difficulties." [63] Instead of such a precise limitation of assistance we have instead the forthright statement by a member of the President's Council of Economic Advisers in the only Republican Administration since 1930 that no "rate of unemployment ought to be called acceptable, because the people who are unemployed certainly do not feel that way about it. So long as there is any possibility of improving the situation I would suggest that we keep improving it." [64] A decade of guarantees to capital values (guarantees of bank deposits, of mortgage loans) and to investments in labor skills and work habits (unemployment insurance) has marked the transition.

By increasing our emphasis on a low unemployment goal we necessarily tend to downgrade the goal of price stability, for the two are in clear conflict—significantly so at some levels of unemployment and some levels of price change. However, American experience suggests that within likely peacetime unemployment ranges the conflict is not as great as might appear. Recent studies indicate that postwar wage changes are largely accounted for by factors other than the unemployment rate.[65]

Suppose we now ask: What is a practicable minimum goal toward which the authorities can aim? Such a goal can be defined as having two elements:[66]

1. Wipe out cyclical unemployment (defined operationally as cutting down the number of these unemployed under fifteen weeks to no more than 3.5 per cent of the labor force).
2. Reduce long-term unemployment (those unemployed over fifteen weeks) to 0.1 per cent of the labor force.

The cyclical unemployment goal proposed above is a simple average of the rates actually achieved in 1948 and in 1956.[67] In both these recent years, production burgeoned, prices were kept tolerably stable, and rising government demand did not dominate the economy. Hence actual experience suggests this figure as a very practicable goal. But we must remember that an annual average rate does not reveal how many different people suffered unemployment; thus the unemployment average for 1956 was 2.5 million, but 14.6 million different workers became unemployed in that prosperity year.[68] Hence the personal adjustments, dangers and discomforts associated even with a 3.5 per cent minimum must be evaluated on the assumption that the equivalent of 20 per cent of the labor force will *become* unemployed during the year.[69]

Such a minimum would be set too low if automation displaced workers at an ever-accelerating rate. Recent experience, however, does not portend major changes in such displacement rates. On the other hand, a more forthright attack on seasonal unemployment, together with the spread of union-management plans that penalize job displacement, are likely to reduce short-term unemployment. Moreover, improved training and counseling in high schools could reduce teen-age unemployment—at present a massive contributor to the substratum of such short-term unemployment. Finally, any

further advances in the use and efficiency of the U.S. Employment
Service should also go toward making a goal of even 3 per cent a not
unreasonable one.

The long-term unemployment component is set below the 0.5 per
cent average of 1948 and 1956. This lower goal recognizes both the
need for and the likely prospect of a much more active labor market policy in depressed areas and industries and among the problem groups which have grown to accept unemployment as a normal
way of life. The social and political problems of West Virginia and
Harlem are increasingly taken as subjects for action. Whatever actions are taken to meet such problems will inevitably involve attempts to train workers for the jobs of the 1960's, and to return
them to productive employment.

The reduction, first to 1948/56 levels and then down to 0.1 per
cent, is hardly a visionary goal: this would still leave an average
of 75,000 workers without jobs for three months or more. (Hence
during the course of any year perhaps a third of a million workers
would have individually suffered such longer periods of unemployment.*) A drop to 1956 levels may come as an incidental result of
general fiscal and monetary policies that raise demand and increase
mobility and job prospects. But further reduction is not likely to
come from such policies, even doubled and tripled.

However, economic policies are inextricably involved with social
and political considerations. And it may be fairly assumed that the
growing concern with area pockets of hard-core unemployment
and with the problems of discrimination and technological displacement will take active form in labor market policies that cut down
the size of this category.

The 3.5 per cent goal to which these components (roughly) add
up involves even more joblessness than the 3.3 per cent average of
1923-29—a span of active advance by private enterprise, of technological creativity, of only minimum government intervention in
the economy.[70] Given the decline of farming since then, a 3.5 per

---

* In 1956 an average of 0.5 million workers were unemployed fifteen weeks
or more in one spell, but five times as many (over 2.6 million workers) lost
a total of fifteen weeks or more during the year in unemployment. Furthermore, over half of the 2.6 million became unemployed at least twice during
the year. This substantial amount of misdirection in job-hunting and choice
should, with an active labor market policy, be reducible without any real cost
either in allocative efficiency and/or inflationary tendencies.

cent national goal implies an unemployment rate in nonfarm labor markets about as high as that prevailing in the days of Calvin Coolidge. Surely the goal for the 1960's should not be a less tolerable one.

NOTES

1. *The Works and Correspondence of David Ricardo,* ed., P. Sraffa (1952), Vol. 5, p. 30.
2. *Ibid.,* p. 302.
3. Philip H. Wicksteed, *Common Sense of Political Economy* (1910), p. 352.
4. Emily Clark Brown, "The Soviet Labor Market," *Industrial and Labor Relations Review* (January 1957), 195.
5. Cf. Robert Myers & J. H. Chandler in President's Committee to Appraise Employment and Unemployment Statistics, *Measuring Employment and Unemployment* (1962) p. 26 (referred to hereafter as the Gordon Report, the Committee's chairman being R. A. Gordon).
6. *Ibid.,* p. 268.
7. Everett Hawkins, in Walter Galenson (ed.), *Labor in Developing Economies* (1962), p. 88.
8. P. Sylos Labini, "La Disoccupazione nelle zone arretrate," *Il Ponte* (November 1957), 1634.
9. This definition is taken from *Employment and Earnings* (October 1963), E-3.
10. The writer has discussed some of these definitional issues at greater length in "Measuring Employment," *Review of Economics and Statistics* (November 1954). Since that time the official series has shifted to the treatment of the temporary layoff group urged in that study, but the issues discussed there continue to be of concern to those using and producing the survey data.
11. Seventh Census of Canada, Monograph No. 11: *Unemployment,* p. 211.
12. Senate of Canada, *Final Report . . . on Manpower and Employment* (June 1961), p. 60.
13. *1940 Census of Population,* Vol. III: *The Labor Force,* Table 5; *Manpower Report of the President* (1963), Table A-8.
14. Wilfred Malenbaum, "Urban Unemployment in India," *Pacific Affairs* (June 1957), 145-46.
15. Walter Kotschnig, *Unemployment in the Learned Professions* (1937).
16. *Manpower Report of the President* (March 1963), p. 43.
17. *1950 Census of Population,* Vol. II, Part 1: *U.S. Summary,* Table 52; *1960 Census of Population: U.S. Summary: General Social and Economic Characteristics,* Table 82.
18. *The 1937 Enumerative Check Census* (Vol. IV, pp. 103–105) also reports the greatest differentials in the North Central region (and Middle Atlantic), but no differentials in the East South Central.
19. *1964 Statistical Abstract,* p. 610.

50   *Stanley Lebergott*

20. *Labor Mobility and Population in Agriculture* (Iowa State University Center for Agricultural and Economic Adjustment, 1961), p. 50.
21. Computed from data in Tables 6 and 12 of the *1950 Census of Population: Population Mobility—Characteristics of Migrants.*
22. *The Labor Market and Employment Security* (October 1952), p. 18.
23. Data from *The Labor Market and Employment Security* (October 1955, October 1959, and October 1963).
24. Data from U.S. Bureau of Labor Statistics, *Employment and Earnings Statistics for the United States, 1909-60*, pp. 12, 40, 421; U.S. Department of Commerce, *U.S. Income and Output*, p. 212.
25. Contract award data as a ratio to population and income appear in Walter Isard and James Ganschow, *Awards of Prime Military Contracts. . . . Fiscal 1960* (Regional Science Research Institute, n.d.), Table 1. Data by income give the same result.
26. Data from Everett Lee, A. R. Miller, C. P. Brainerd and R. A. Easterlin, *Population Redistribution and Economic Growth, United States, 1870-1950* (1957), Table P-1.
27. *Ibid.*, p. 114, deducting net in migration from the population at each point. Data for those aged ten and over.
28. See the discussion in any standard text: e.g., Melvin Reder, *Labor in a Growing Economy* (1957). Chap. 17. On the relevance of policy choice, *v.* Neil Chamberlain in Joint Economic Committee, *Hearings on Employment, Growth, and Price Levels,* Part 8, pp. 2703 ff.
29. Joint Economic Committee, *New Views on Automation* (1960) p. 248.
30. Senate Committee on Labor and Public Welfare, *Nation's Manpower Revolution,* Part 5 (1963), p. 1468.
31. The most extended perceptive review is by Bert Hickman, *Growth and Stability in the Postwar Economy* (1960). A comprehensive review of one downturn appears in Geoffrey Moore, "The 1957-58 Business Contraction," *American Economic Review* (May 1959).
32. Deflated GNP components as estimated by the U.S. Department of Commerce *Economic Report of the President* (1964), pp. 208, 209. Capacity utilization estimates of Frank de Leeuw, from American Statistical Association, *1963 Proceedings of the Business and Economic Section,* p. 226.
33. The 1900 figure is from the *1900 Census of Population,* Vol. X, p. 381. It appears to be roughly comparable with the later data, which are from *New Views on Automation* (1960) p. 177, statement by the Director of the Census. Cf. Solomon Fabricant, *Employment in Manufacturing,* p. 204.
34. Industry detail from the *Censuses of Manufacturers,* as follows: *1958 Census,* Vol. I, pp. 1–18; *1947 Census,* Vol. 1, p. 90. Household and farm estimated from product detail in the *1947 Product Supplement,* p. 162; Vol. I, p. 90; *1929 Census,* pp. 1108, 1135; Fabricant, *op. cit.,* p. 204; *1899 Census,* Vol. X, Part 4, p. 366. Total machinery from testimony of the Director of the Census in JEC, *New Views on Automation,* p. 175.
35. Productivity estimates of John Kendrick, from U.S. Bureau of the Census, *Historical Statistics,* p. 599 and National Bureau of Economic Research, *Forty-second Annual Report* (June 1962), p. 40.
36. *1940 Census of Population: Occupational Characteristics,* Table 4, and U.S. Bureau of Labor Statistics Special Labor Force Report No. 30: *Educational Attainment of Workers* (March 1962), p. 509.
37. *1950 Census of Population: Occupation by Industry,* Table 2; *1960 Census of Population: Occupation by Industry,* Table 2.

38. James R. Bright, "Does Automation Raise Skill Requirements?" *Harvard Business Review* (July-August 1958), 97. For a sharply opposed view, *cf.* Roger Bolz in *New Views on Automation* (1960), especially p. 23.
39. Estimated in Stanley Lebergott, "Labor Force and Employment, 1800-1960," *Studies in Income and Wealth*, Vol. XXIX.
40. Fabricant, *op. cit.*, p. 331.
41. We rely on two analyses by Ewan Clague and Leon Greenberg, as reported in American Assembly, *Automation and Technological Change*, John Dunlop (ed.), p. 126 and Senate Committee on Labor and Public Welfare, *op. cit.*, Part 5, p. 1586, as slightly revised in later work. The data used apply to production workers in manufacturing.
42. Cf. the section on "External Economies, Uncertainty and Wages," in Stanley Lebergott, *Manpower in Economic Growth* (1964), pp. 241 ff.
43. Thomas Kennedy, *Automation Funds and Displaced Workers* (1962), pp. 340, 344.
44. See, *inter alia*, the extensive discussion in Clarence Long, "Prosperity Unemployment and Its Relation to Economic Growth and Inflation," *American Economic Association, Papers and Proceedings* (May 1960), and the report by Congressman MacGregor in the *Congressional Record* for July 25, 1961.
45. *Congressional Record*, July 25, 1961.
46. *Congressional Record*, August 3, 1961.
47. An excellent and more perceptive review of unemployment than hundreds of others, "Unemployment in 1937," appeared in *Fortune* (November 1937).
48. *Digest of Annual Reports of State Boards for Vocational Education to the Office of Education . . . Fiscal year ended June 30, 1962.* We use data for day classes from pp. 23, 34, 40, 50.
49. The House Committee on Education and Labor, 88th Congress, 1st Session, *Report 861.* The most basic report is the comprehensive *Report of the Secretary of Labor, Manpower, Research, and Training under the Manpower Development and Training Act, March 1964.*
50. Robert Goodwin, Deputy Manpower Administrator for Operations, in Senate Committee on Labor and Public Welfare, *op. cit.*, Part 2, pp. 344, 357.
51. Testimony of Seymour Wolfbein, Director, Office of Manpower, Automation, and Training, in *Nation's Manpower Revolution*, Part 2, p. 561.
52. Testimony of Samuel Ganz in *ibid.*, Part 4, p. 1080.
53. Nassau Senior, quoted in George Hilton, "The Controversy Concerning Relief for the Hand-Loom Weavers," *Explorations in Entrepreneurial History* (Winter 1964), p. 166.
54. If one wants to emphasize liquidity preference as constituting a sufficient motive for holding cash then the argument would be still stronger.
55. U.S. Bureau of Labor Statistics Special Labor Force Report No. 35: Gertrude Bancroft and Stuart Garfinkle, *Job Mobility in 1961.* From Table A in this report we estimate the number who changed jobs without looking for work and total job changers; from Table I, jobs left. The ratio of one to the other, when applied to the 4,480,000, yields 7,260,000. U.S. Bureau of Labor Statistics Special Labor Force Report 29, Table 1, gives an estimate of persons with two jobs—*not* included in the above data. This category has averaged at least 3 million in each of six surveys since 1956, being 3.3 million in May 1962. We take 3.0 as a minimum annual average figure for 1961.
56. U.S. Bureau of Labor Statistics Special Labor Force Report No. 31:

Labor Force and Employment, 1960-62, Table D-5, reports 2.8 million nonfarm employees working part-time for economic reasons. About 35.8 per cent of the wage and salary workers in agriculture worked under thirty-five hours (the full-time cut-off point) according to Table D-2. But had the proportion of part-time self-employed workers (e.g., 24.2 per cent) applied to this group, about 200,000 fewer workers would have been in the short-time group. We take this difference to measure involuntary part-time work by farm employees—i.e., not associated with part-time work on account of weather, desire for part-time work, and so on.

57. U.S. Bureau of the Census, *Current Population Reports,* P-50, No. 36: *Experience of workers at their current jobs* (January 1951) Table 1; U.S. Bureau of Labor Statistics Special Labor Force Report No. 36: *Job Tenure of American Workers* (January 1963) gives data for a much more recent, but a slow-growth period. A marked freezing of the labor force, in response to this slackening, is apparent, immobility increasing with unemployment.

58. We compute age at entrance by weighting the proportions in the labor force for each age interval using data from the *1950 Census of Population: Employment and Personal Characteristics,* Table 2. We assume that the participation rates for age twenty-five to twenty-nine represent the full participation possibilities for the young, recognizing variations in health, gross unemployability, and so on. For age at exit we use sixty-two, given the 42.6-year work expectancy for those at age twenty in 1960; 43.1 in 1950. (For the latter see the OMAT estimate in Senate Committee on Labor and Public Welfare, *op. cit.* (August 1963).

59. A more recent Census survey shows a marked rise from 3.9 to 5.7 years on his present job by the typical male worker, suggesting the extent to which the labor force freezes in response to slackened growth, slower hiring. U.S. Bureau of Labor Statistics Special Labor Force Report No. 36: *Job Tenure of American Workers,* Table F. On the other hand heavy firings in deep depression tended to increase the number of jobs held by Philadelphia toolmakers. Cf. Carol Brainerd in Gladys L. Palmer, *et. al., The Reluctant Job Changer* (1962), p. 87.

60. U.S. Bureau of Labor Statistics Special Labor Force Report No. 35: *Job Mobility in 1961,* Table J. The reported total includes some lesser causes, but probably excludes admissions of worker firings for personal reasons.

61. Commission on Money and Credit, *Money and Credit* (1961), p. 28.

62. Herbert Hoover, *Lincoln's Day Address, 1931.* In the prior October the President stated that he had "been in communication with some of the governors in development of methods by which the federal government can further supplement assistance to their organizations," the results of the survey he expected to give "valuable suggestive material and information for the winter." Quoted in E. P. Hayes, *Activities of the President's Emergency Committee for Employment* (1936), p. 7.

63. Quoted in *ibid.,* p. 2.

64. Joint Economic Committee, *Hearings: Review of the Report of the Commission on Money and Credit* (August 1961), p. 422.

65. See W. Bowen and R. A. Berry, "Unemployment Conditions and Movements of the Money Wage Level," *Review of Economics and Statistics* (May 1963); R. R. France, "Wages, Unemployment, and Prices in the United States, 1890-1932, 1947-1957," *Industrial and Labor Relations Review* (January 1962); Otto Eckstein and Thomas Wilson, "The Determina-

tion of Money Wages in American Industry," *Quarterly Journal of Economics* (August 1962).

66. Note that these percentages differ from those to which I referred in the Proceedings of the Industrial Relations Research Association for 1961, and in Commission on Money and Credit, *Inflation, Growth and Unemployment* (1964). The difference (even ignoring the qualifications made in these reports) is that I was speaking only of actions appropriate to the fiscal and monetary authorities, whereas here the goal is one encompassing actions by the labor market agencies as well.

67. Data adjusted for changes in concept.

68. U.S. Bureau of the Census, *Annual Report on the Labor Force, 1956,* Table 16, indicates that 1,214,000 workers on the average were unemployed less than five weeks in 1956. Since this group automatically leaves the "under-five-week" category by the time of next month's enumeration, multiplying by 12 gives us the number of entrances to unemployment during the year.

69. In 1956 there were an average of 2.5 million unemployed during the year, 10.0 million persons who became unemployed at some time during the year, and (because many workers became unemployed more than once during the year) about 14.6 million entrances to unemployment. Data from U.S. Bureau of the Census, *Current Population Reports,* Series P-50, No. 77, p. 2; No. 72, p. 30; entrances calculated as in footnote above.

70. This is the entire period from the end of the post-World War I depression to the beginning of the depression of the 1930's, and actually includes two recessions, those of 1924 and of 1927.

PART I

The Present Dilemma

AUTOMATION, JOBS, AND MANPOWER

Charles C. Killingsworth

Charles C. Killingsworth is Professor of Labor and Industrial Relations at Michigan State University. His study and experience encompass exposure to major problems and responsibilities which anyone purporting to comment on labor market problems should ardently desire, but which few would, in fact, welcome—as permanent umpire for Bethlehem Steel and the United Steel Workers, for Ford and the United Auto Workers, and as Chairman of the National Wage Stabilization Board.

. . . When a major labor-saving invention is introduced in an industry which is in its rapid-growth stage—its adolescence—the invention may help to spur further rapid growth, especially through price cuts, and total employment in the industry may increase substantially. This is the historical pattern which prompts many people to argue that "machines make jobs." But the fact is that when an industry has reached maturity—for example, when there is already one car for each three people—it just is not possible to achieve further dramatic increases in sales, even with the largest price cuts within the realm of reason. The improved productivity made possible by labor-saving machines simply enables the industry to keep up with the normal growth of the market while employing fewer production workers. This is what happened in a number of our major industries in the 1950's.

Look across the whole range of consumer goods and you will see that our mass consumption society has done a highly effective job

From a statement made before the Senate Subcommittee on Employment and Manpower and reprinted from the Committee's *Nation's Manpower Revolution*, Part 5 (1963).

of supplying the wants of the great majority of consumers.* About
99.5 per cent of the homes that are wired for electricity have electric refrigerators; 93 per cent have television sets; 83 per cent have
electric washing machines; and we have even more radios than
homes. The only sharply rising sales curve in the consumer-durables
field today is that of the electric can-opener industry. The electric
toothbrush and electric hairbrush industries are starting to grow
rapidly, too. But the growth of employment in these new "industries" will not offset the declines in the older, larger consumer goods
industries.

The doctrine that "machines make jobs," to the extent that it
rests on research rather than faith—is drawn primarily from studies
of the periods 1899-1937 and 1899-1953. These were mainly years
when the growth potential of most markets for goods was still very
great. I think that it is a major source of error to assume that the
markets of our great mass-production industries will grow at the
same prodigious rate in the second half of the twentieth century
that they achieved in the first half. Without that kind of growth
rate, the doctrine that "machines make jobs" will surely be as obsolete as the Model T.

We can get some perspective on our present situation by considering the basic causes for the booming prosperity which most of Western Europe and Japan are now enjoying. Those countries are in
the early growth stages of the mass-consumption society. Their
ratios of automobiles to population, electric refrigerators to houses,
and so on, are generally comparable to our ratios in the 1920's (or
earlier). At their present rates of growth, it will be several decades
before they achieve our degree of saturation of markets. So automation is having a different impact there.

* I am not unaware of the "vast unmet needs" (to use the familiar phrase)
in such fields as education and housing. I have more to say about education
below. The housing needs are found almost entirely in "the other America"—
the 20 or 30 per cent of the population with incomes so low that these people
do not realistically provide a market for anything more than the barest es-
sentials. Unless their incomes rise dramatically—and there is no apparent reason
to expect this to happen—their housing and other needs will remain unmet.
This is not, of course, a situation which we should complacently accept; but we
are not doing very much about it. The point here is the elementary one that in
our society "vast unmet needs" do not equal vast markets without purchasing
power in the hands of those who have the needs.

I do not mean to suggest that all consumer markets in the United States are approaching saturation and that consumers will soon be buying only replacements for what they already have. One of the few things that we can predict with reasonable certainty in economics is that as consumers' incomes rise, their spending will rise, too. But our history reveals some long-run changes in the patterns of consumer spending. These changes have an important effect on patterns of employment. . . .

. . . The United States is the only country in the world in which the jobs in services outnumber the jobs in goods industries.

Will the growth of jobs in the services offset the loss of jobs in goods industries? This kind of offset is possible, but by no means inevitable. We cannot safely accept the convenient assumption of economic theory that all labor is homogeneous, and the conclusion that only inertia or ignorance can impede the free flow of laborers from one industry to another as the patterns of consumer spending change. The displaced assembly-line worker may be readily adaptable to work in a filling station; he may be much less acceptable as a clerk in a department store; and, without years of training, he cannot qualify as a teacher or a nurse. Adapting the labor force to changes in the supply of jobs is a matter of crucial importance in our society today. I will return to this point shortly.

The economic environment today is so different from that of forty or fifty years ago that simply more of the same kinds of technological change that we experienced in the first half of the century would have a different impact now. But automation differs in some respects from most of the earlier technological changes.

One major difference is the much broader applicability of automation. The steam engine had a number of uses, but mainly in factories and in transportation. The cotton gin, the spinning jenny, the linotype, and others had a substantial impact, but each in only one industry. The examples that I have already given of automation applications illustrate the versatility of the techniques. Computer technology in particular seems likely to invade almost every area of industrial activity.

A related difference is that automation appears to be spreading more rapidly than most major technological changes of the past. It is difficult, if not impossible, to measure the diffusion of technology in quantitative terms, of course. But I find these facts suggestive: About a century was required for the general adoption of the steam engine in those activities where it could be employed; the comparable timespan for electric power was about fifty years. The first automatic accounting systems were installed in banks some seven or eight years ago. Today, about half of the banks are in the process of converting to this system. When the first large-scale computers were introduced early in the 1950's, there were estimates that only about ten or fifteen of them would ever be needed in the entire United States. Today, nearly 4000 fully transistorized computers are in use, and the number on order is about double that, so that in two or three years we will have about three times as many in use as we have today.*

A third characteristic of automation techniques is that, to a much greater extent than past technologies, they are the product of the laboratory scientist rather than the production man. In other words, the importance of pure science as a source of invention has greatly increased. In the days of Henry Ford I, it was reasonably accurate to say that "necessity is the mother of invention." At the end of 1912, Ford had a huge backlog of orders which created an urgent necessity for an invention that would greatly increase his production. So Henry Ford—a talented tinkerer without any formal training in science or engineering—invented the assembly line. In the days of Henry Ford II, there is no great pressure of sales on production facilities. In the Nation as a whole, about 20 per cent of our productive capacity is idle. The automatic refining unit and the automatic steel mill were not invented because of an urgent demand for vastly larger quantities of oil and steel. These inventions were the byproduct of the very rapid growth of scientific knowledge in our generation. In the last half of the century, we are often finding that "invention is the mother of necessity." . . .

* If automation is spreading as rapidly as I think, why don't our productivity figures show substantial increase? In the first place, the rate of improvement in output per man-hour has been somewhat higher in recent years than the long-run trend (about at the level of the 1920's, in fact). In the second place, as I have already suggested, most automation installations require a very large investment of man-hours in preparatory work; changing these man-hours against current output undoubtedly results in an understatement of the current rate of productivity improvement. The operation of the economy at considerably less than optimum levels of output has also helped to hold down the productivity figures.

Automation, especially in its advanced forms, fundamentally changes the man-machine relation. Such a change is not unprecedented in economic history. The assembly line, as it replaced earlier techniques, helped to create literally millions of simple, repetitive jobs that could be learned in a few hours or a few days. Anybody who had two hands, two eyes, and a capacity to endure monotony could do the work.

Today we have the electric eye, the iron hand, the tin ear, and the electronic brain. We also have the know-how to tie them together in self-regulating systems that can perform an enormous variety of jobs. There are two major results. One is a great reduction in the number of simple, repetitive jobs where all you need is your five senses and an untrained mind. The other result is a great increase in the number of jobs involved in designing, engineering, programming and administering these automatic production systems. Industry needs many more scientists, engineers, mathematicians, and other highly trained people, and many fewer blue-collar workers.

. . . Between 1957 and 1962 . . . manufacturing production workers declined by nearly a million . . . , while nonproduction workers increased by about a third of a million. The net change was a reduction of about 600,000 in employment.

Not all of the increase in white-collar employment in manufacturing was due to automation, of course, and not all of the newly hired employees were scientists and engineers. But the changing composition of employment was partly due to automation. Moreover, what happened from 1957 to 1962 was the continuation of a postwar trend. . . . Throughout the 1920's, the ratio between production and nonproduction workers in manufacturing fluctuated . . . around . . . 20 per cent. The great depression and World War II temporarily affected the ratio; at the outset of the depression, the blue-collar workers were laid off before the white-collar workers were, and in the war salesmen and clerks were drafted while blue-collar workers were added. By about 1951, the prewar ratio of about one white-collar worker to four blue-collar workers had been re-established. But as automation gathered momentum during the 1950's, the ratio continued to change. It is now at about 26 per cent and the trend is still strongly upward. Generally, the most highly automated industries have the highest ratio of white-collar workers.

In chemicals and petroleum, for example, the ratio is 40 per cent. In an economy in which so many patterns are changing rapidly, broad averages and grand totals may conceal more than they reveal. I think that this is especially true of the effects of automation and the concomitant changes of today. Let us take as an example the . . . persistent upward trend in total employment—from 58 million jobs in 1949 to more than 68 million in 1963. This great increase is another piece of evidence often cited by those who claim that "machines make jobs." But there is another side to this coin. . . . Unemployment crept upward during the latter part of this period— first two notches up, then one notch down, and then another two notches up. In 1951-53, the average was about a 3 per cent rate of unemployment. In 1962-63, the average has been almost double that, or between 5.5 and 6 per cent.

It is not self-evident from these figures that any part of this creeping unemployment problem is due to automation or other basic changes in the patterns of the economy. There is eminent authority to the contrary. The President's Council of Economic Advisers has repeatedly declared that automation and "structural unemployment" are not responsible for the gradual creep of unemployment above the 4 per cent level of 1957.

I think that it can be demonstrated that the Council is the victim of a half-truth. The lagging growth rate is only a part of the problem, and it may not be the most important part. The fundamental effect of automation on the labor market is to "twist" the pattern of demand—that is, it pushes down the demand for workers with little training while pushing up the demand for workers with large amounts of training. The shift from goods to services is a second major factor which twists the labor market in the same way. There are some low-skilled, blue-collar jobs in service-producing industries; but the most rapidly growing parts of the service sector are health care and education, both of which require a heavy preponderance of highly trained people.

I have already presented some figures showing the changing patterns of demand for labor. These changing patterns of demand would not create labor market imbalance, however, unless changes in the supply of labor lagged behind. We turn now to the figures which show that such a lag has in fact developed.

Table 1 shows the relationship between rates of unemployment

Table 1

Education and unemployment, April 1950 and March 1962
(males, 18 and over)

Years of school completed	Unemployment rates		Percentage change, 1950-62
	1950	1962	
0-7	8.4	9.2	+9.5
8	6.6	7.5	+13.6
9-11	6.9	7.8	+13.0
12	4.6	4.8	+4.3
13-15	4.1	4.0	−2.4
16 or more	2.2	1.4	−36.4
All groups	*6.2*	*6.0*	*−3.2*

and levels of education of males eighteen and over in two years—
1950 and 1962.

The over-all unemployment rate was substantially the same in
both years—6.2 in 1950, and 6.0 in 1962. But there was a redistribution of unemployment between these two years. The unemployment rates at the top of the educational attainment ladder went
down, while the rates at the middle and lower rungs of the ladder
went up substantially. The most significant figure in this table, I
think, is the one showing the very large decrease in the unemployment rate of college graduates.

In a sense, these unemployment figures are only the part of the
iceberg that is above the water. For a better understanding of their
significance, we must consider also the changes in demand and supply that took place at the various educational levels between 1950
and 1962. . . . The number of persons with zero to seven years of
education in the labor force declined very greatly from 1950 to 1962;
but the jobs held by this group declined even more, so that its unemployment rate went up. The supply of labor with eight years
of education also decreased, and the demand for this group decreased
even more, and its unemployment rate increased by more than the
increase in rate for the zero to seven classification. We see a different relationship between supply and demand in the nine to eleven
years of education group. Supply increased; demand also increased,
but by less than the increase in supply, so that a higher unemploy-

ment rate resulted here too. The high school graduates (twelve years of education) fared somewhat better. There was a substantial increase in supply in this group, and demand also kept pace, so that this group's unemployment rate went up by less than the rates of the less educated groups. The groups with college training were quite fortunate, especially those with at least four years of college. The supply of men with thirteen to fifteen years of education increased by almost 50 per cent, but the jobs for them increased by slightly more, so that their unemployment rate (which was already low) went down slightly. The experience of the group with sixteen or more years of education was particularly striking. The supply of men in this group increased by 75 per cent, but the jobs for them increased even more than that, so that their unemployment rate went down by more than a third.

It is important to note that all of the improvement in the unemployment situation in 1962, as compared with 1950, was concentrated in the elite group of our labor force—the approximately 20 per cent with college training. In all of the other categories, which have about 80 per cent of the labor force, unemployment rates were substantially higher in 1962 than in 1950. These figures, I contend, substantiate the thesis that the patterns of demand for labor have been twisted faster than the patterns of supply have changed, and that as a result we had a substantially greater degree of labor market imbalance in 1962 than in 1950.

It seems probable that worsening employment prospects for a particular group over a long period would force down the labor force participation rate—i.e., would squeeze a number of people out of the labor market altogether, in the sense that they would give up the continuing, active search for jobs. Conversely, it seems probable that improving employment prospects would tend to pull more people into the labor market and thus to raise the labor force participation rate. These two trends are indeed observable since 1950. The squeezing out of people at the lower end of the educational ladder and the pulling in of people at the upper end is another manifestation of the labor market twist. Table 2 presents the pertinent figures for males.

The important point that I want to make with these figures is that in all likelihood the official unemployment statistics substantially understate the size of the labor surplus of men with limited

Table 2

Labor force participation rates and educational attainment,
April 1950 and March 1962
(males, 18 and over)

Years of school completed	Labor force participation rates		Percentage change in rate, 1950-62
	1950	1962	
0-4	74.6	58.2	−22.0
5-7	85.0	74.6	−14.4
8	88.1	78.2	−12.7
9-11	92.1	88.8	−3.9
12	94.0	90.7	−3.7
13-15	79.6	83.0	+5.4
16 or more	92.1	92.3	+0.2
All groups	*87.6*	*83.5*	*−4.7*

education. If we found jobs for most of those now officially re-ported as unemployed, the news of improving opportunities would undoubtedly bring back into the labor force many men who are not now counted as members of it. Unfortunately, we cannot count on the same flexibility of supply at the top of the educational scale. Even the most extreme pressures of demand cannot pull the partici-pation rate much above 98 or 99 per cent, which (as just stated) is the current rate in some college-trained age groups.

Our over-all unemployment rate has now been above 5 per cent for more than five years, and we cannot be sure what effects a sub-stantial increase in spending by consumers, businesses, and gov-ernment (i.e., an increase in aggregate demand) would have on the patterns of employment, unemployment, and labor force participa-tion just discussed. Many respected economists believe, as one of them once put it, that the hard core of unemployment is made of ice, not rock, and that it would melt away if over-all demand rose high enough. As already noted, the Council of Economic Advisers has virtually guaranteed that the administration's tax cut program—which in its current version would put about $11 billion in the hands of consumers and businesses—would reduce unemployment to an "interim target" rate of 4 per cent by 1966. This line of reason-ing assumes (either implicitly or sometimes explicitly) that no serious bottlenecks of labor supply would appear before the achievement of the over-all unemployment rate of 4 per cent. I seriously question the validity of this critically important assumption under the labor market conditions of today and the foreseeable future.

The benefits of a decline in the over-all rate of unemployment appear to be quite unevenly distributed among the educational attainment groups that we have been considering. The year 1957 was the last one in which we had an unemployment rate as low as 4 per cent. It is instructive to see how the patterns of unemployment changed from 1950, when the over-all rate was above 6 per cent, to 1957, and then again to 1962, which had about the same over-all rate as 1950. This comparison is made in two forms in Table 3. This table shows the actual unemployment rates for the

Table 3

Actual and relative unemployment rates by educational attainment,
April 1950, March 1957, and March 1962
(males, 18 and over)

Years of school completed	Unemployment rates					
	Actual percentages			Relative[1]		
	1950	1957	1962	1950	1957	1962
0-7	8.4	6.9	9.2	154	203	170
8	6.6	4.4	7.5	108	110	132
9-11	6.9	4.7	7.3	115	120	142
12	4.6	3.0	4.8	70	67	75
13-15	4.1	2.7	4.0	64	64	65
16 or more	2.2	.6	1.4	34	14	21
All groups	*6.2*	*4.1*	*6.0*	[1]	[1]	[1]

[1] The relative unemployment rate is the ratio between the percentage unemployment rate for a given educational attainment group and the percentage unemployment rate for all other groups at the same point in time.

various educational attainment groups in those three years, and it also expresses the unemployment rate for each group in each of the three years as a ratio of the rate for all of the other groups combined. (Thus, the zero to seven years of education group had an unemployment rate about 50 per cent higher than all other groups combined in 1950; its rate was more than double the rate for all other groups in 1957; and its rate was 70 per cent higher in 1962.)

Clearly, unemployment at the bottom of the educational scale was relatively unresponsive to general increases in the demand for labor, while there was very strong responsiveness at the top of the educational scale. The percentage unemployment rate for college graduates in 1957 merits close attention. It was an almost incredible 0.6 per cent. I have queried the experts in the Bureau of Labor Statistics on this figure, and they assure me that they have no less confidence in it than in the other 1957 figures. Surely a figure as low as that represents what is sometimes called "overfull" employment—i.e., demand which seriously exceeds supply.

Bear in mind that the unemployment rates for the lower educational attainment groups (those with 80 per cent of the men) are now higher than in 1950, and that the unemployment rate for college graduates is now substantially lower than in 1950. Also bear in mind that the labor force participation rate figures strongly suggest a large and growing "reserve army"—which is not counted among the unemployed—at the lower educational levels, and that there is no evidence of any such reserve of college-trained men. Finally, bear in mind the differences between the lower end of the educational scale and the upper end in responsiveness to over-all decreases in the unemployment rate.

When you put all of these considerations together, I believe that you are ineluctably led to the conclusion that long before we could get down to an over-all unemployment rate as low as 4 per cent, we would have a severe shortage of workers at the top of the educational ladder. This shortage would be a bottleneck to further expansion of employment. I cannot pinpoint the level at which the bottleneck would begin to seriously impede expansion; but, on the basis of the relationships revealed by Table 3, it seems reasonable to believe that we could not get very far below a 5 per cent over-all unemployment level without hitting that bottleneck.

The most fundamental conclusion that emerges from my analysis is that automation and the changing pattern of consumer wants have greatly increased the importance of investment in human beings as a factor in economic growth. More investment in plant and equipment, without very large increases in our investment in human beings, seems certain to enlarge the surplus of underdeveloped manpower and to create a shortage of the highly developed manpower needed to design, install, and man modern production facilities. The Manpower Development and Training Act is aptly named, soundly conceived, and well administered. This program was not originally intended to provide general literacy training as such; separate legislation was proposed for that purpose but was not adopted. Experience under the Manpower Development and Training Act has shown how essential literacy training is as a prerequisite for specific occupational training. (In 1962, 40 per cent of the unemployed males had eight or fewer years of schooling, but only 13 per cent of the Manpower Development and Training Act male trainees had that little education.) If the House agrees with action already taken by the Senate to provide literacy training under the Manpower Development and Training Act, the original scope of the program will be broadened in a highly desirable way. But I doubt that even the most enthusiastic supporters of the Manpower Development and Training Act program (and I count myself among them) would argue that its present or projected size is really commensurate with the size of the job to be done. We ought to be thinking in terms of helping two or three times as many people as this program is now expected to reach. I do not imply any criticism of Congress in this comment, because it is my strong impression that dollars are not the limiting factor in the development of the Manpower Development and Training Act program. The real shortage in most areas, I believe, is trained manpower—specifically, qualified instructors and program administrators. It would be pointless to double or triple the appropriations for the program if the extra money could not be spent, and I doubt that it could be. Here we have an example of a present shortage of highly trained manpower, a shortage that limits the possibility of investment to remedy the educational deficiencies of the past.

Let us consider another, somewhat similar example. As we have all heard over and over again, the outlook for high school dropouts is bleak indeed. Exhortations, no matter how well meant, are not going to cure this problem, and neither will the token fund set aside by President Kennedy for grants to local units for experimental programs in this area. But here again dollars alone are not the answer. We need many more highly skilled teachers, counselors, and social workers. These, too, are in very short supply. Many other present shortages of highly trained manpower, in the private sector of the economy as well as in the public, could be cited. Unquestionably these shortages would be intensified and new ones would appear if we moved closer to full utilization of our economic potential.

To my mind, the greatest shortcoming of the administration's program for reducing unemployment is the failure to recognize the crucial need to break the trained manpower bottleneck. I recognize that the administration has recommended what many people regard as very ambitious measures for federal aid to higher education. But even if these measures were accepted in their entirety, it is most unlikely that they would suffice to break the present and prospective bottlenecks in the supply of highly educated manpower. I have proposed (in an as yet unpublished essay) that we make provisions for loans to college students up to a maximum of $12,000, with a repayment period as long as forty years, at a subsidized interest rate of 2 per cent. Repayment should be on the basis of a flat percentage of income—a kind of social security system in reverse. Others may think of better solutions; the means are less important than the end which is to make higher education readily available to all who can benefit from it.

I would give a considerably higher priority to the stimulation of investment in human beings than I would to such measures as the proposed tax cut. But I would still rate the tax cut as important. Denying that the tax cut is the "ultimate weapon" against unemployment is not denying that it can make some contribution to the reduction of unemployment. After all, even to get below a 5 per cent unemployment rate would be a considerable achievement today. But a really effective attack on the complex problem of unemployment requires a whole arsenal of powerful weapons.

And we don't have all the time in the world. Human history has been described as a race between education and catastrophe. In the past dozen years, education has been falling behind in that race.

EMPLOYMENT AND MANPOWER

Walter W. Heller

Walter Heller has been Chairman of the Council of Economic Advisers while on leave from the University of Minnesota's Department of Economics. He has also been an economist in the U.S. Treasury (dealing with federal-state relations); adviser to the Military government in Germany; and financial adviser to King Hussein of Jordan. This unusually rich background has undoubtedly been serviceable, if not in fact essential, for dealing with the vast range of problems and personalities with which the nation's chief economist must cope. This selection is taken from a major statement prepared for the Senate Subcommittee on Employment and Manpower, with additions from the Council of Economic Advisers' Annual Report for 1964.

Recent discussions may have generated an impression of greater disagreement among the nation's economists about the origins and solutions of the employment problem than actually exists. For in fact, the great majority of those who have studied the matter carefully would agree with the Administration's view that our excessive unemployment today cannot be traced to a single cause nor eliminated by a single cure. Rather, it has a mixture of causes which must be dealt with by a mixture—an amalgam—of cures.

One problem, and a central one, is that total expenditures in the economy—total demand for goods and services—are not sufficient to generate an adequate total number of jobs. We can, for convenience, call this kind of unemployment "demand-shortage" unemployment. In our view, demand-shortage unemployment can and must be attacked by vigorous policies—principally tax reduction—to raise the total demand for goods and services.

From the *Economic Report of the President, January 1964.*

Another problem is that the characteristics of our available workers—their locations, skills, education, training, race, sex, age, and so on—do not fully match the characteristics employers are seeking in filling the jobs that are available (or that would be available at full employment). In a dynamic, changing economy there is always some of this mismatching, and we call the unemployment that results from it "frictional." But when the pockets of such unemployment become large and stubborn—especially when they impose chronic burdens on particular disadvantaged groups and regions, we speak of the unemployment problem as "structural."

This type of unemployment is also a serious problem, which requires major policy actions to overcome its corrosive efforts. Structural problems are not new. And the available evidence does not show that the proportion of our total unemployment problem that we label "structural" has increased significantly, nor that its character has materially changed. But this in no way diminishes the need for attacking these structural problems with vigorous policies—principally education, training and retraining, and special regional programs—to match the supply of labor skills more closely to the changing demand for labor skills.

Along with demand-shortage and structural unemployment, one also hears a great deal about the problem of "technological" unemployment—of men being put out of work by machines and, more particularly, by the process which has come to be called *automation*. This is, indeed, a serious and continuing problem. But two points should be emphasized at the outset.

First, "technological" unemployment is not a third form of unemployment, separate from the other two; rather, it expresses itself through these other forms. Technological change causes obsolescence of skills and therefore produces some of the mismatching between available workers and jobs that we call "structural" unemployment. Moreover, by raising output per worker, technological change is one of the principal sources of growth in our *potential* total output or GNP—which, if not matched by corresponding growth in *actual* GNP, opens a gap in demand and thereby causes demand-shortage unemployment.

Second, those who maintain that the economy now faces a problem of "technological" unemployment that is somehow new and more formidable than in the past, implicitly assert that the rate of technological change has recently speeded up. Unless this is the case, the problem is not new—it has always been with us and has not proved to be a long-run problem for the economy as a whole. The continuing process of rapid technological change, which has constituted the very core of the American economy's strength and progressiveness for at least one hundred fifty years, has always put particular workers and businesses out of jobs and required particular adjustments that have been difficult and sometimes painful. It poses a new general problem for the economy only if technological change becomes so rapid that the demand adjustments and labor market adjustments it requires cannot be accomplished by the economic processes of the past. . . .

These, then—demand-shortage elements, structural elements, and a possible aggravation of both by accelerated technological change —are the principal ingredients of the unemployment problem. . . . It would be unwise and imprudent to ignore any of these ingredients either in diagnosing the problem or in prescribing remedies.

The primary attack on high unemployment must be through fiscal measures to speed the growth of total demand and thereby to create new job opportunities. But this need not—indeed, must not—impede a simultaneous attack on our stubborn structural problems. The two approaches are not merely complementary; they are mutually reinforcing. On the one hand, training and other programs to facilitate labor mobility can ease and speed the process by which demand-stimulated increases in output are translated into increases in employment. On the other, since structural maladjustments tend to flourish in slack markets, a vigorous expansion in demand helps cut structural problems down to size.

UNEMPLOYMENT AND TAX REDUCTION

The American economy has been plagued with persistently excessive unemployment for six years. The unemployment rate has been 5 per cent or more for 71 consecutive months. Since 1957, it has averaged 6 per cent. . . . Although GNP rose from $556.8 billion in the third quarter of 1962 to $588.5 billion in the third quarter of 1963, the unemployment rate remained the same in both quarters. . . . The persistence of this high level of unemployment is sometimes cited as evidence of structural difficulties which will blunt the

effect of the proposed $11 billion tax cut. . . . But . . . the road
to 4 per cent unemployment is clearly open to demand-powered
measures:

1. The pre-1957 postwar performance of the U.S. economy gives ample
   evidence of its ability to achieve 4 per cent and even lower levels of
   unemployment without excessive strain.
2. The availability of 1.1 million excess unemployed workers (even by
   the modest 4 per cent criterion and not counting the labor force dropouts resulting from slack job opportunities) and of substantial excess
   capacity (even after large gains, the average operating rate in manufacturing is running at only 87 per cent of capacity) demonstrates that
   we are still suffering from a serious shortage of consumer and investment demand.
3. There are virtually no signs of economic tension, of the barriers that
   would divert the force of demand stimulus away from higher output,
   more jobs, and higher incomes into higher prices—there are no visible
   bottlenecks in the economy, wage-rate increases have been the most
   moderate in the postwar period, and the record of price stability in
   recent years has been outstanding.

. . . The most notable difference between the pre-1957 and post-
1957 periods is found in the strength of market demand. In the first
postwar decade, markets were strong. Backlogs of consumer demand
had to be worked off. The demands of the Korean conflict had to be
met. Outmoded plants and equipment had to be replaced or modern-
ized, and capacity had to be enlarged. Deficiencies in housing, office
facilities, and public works had to be made up.

But 1957 marked a watershed. In the ensuing period, demand has
slackened at a time when our labor force growth has been accelerating in response to the postwar jump in the birth rate. Business
fixed investment dropped off from 10-11 per cent of the GNP to
only 9 per cent—indeed, the level of such investment in 1962 barely
struggled back to its level in 1956, while GNP was rising by nearly
one fifth (both in constant prices).

Thus, the clearest and most striking change since 1957 is the
weakening of demand. So the clearest and most urgent need today
is to remove the overburden of taxation which is retarding the
growth in demand to full employment levels. Income tax rates
enacted to finance war and fight inflation—though reduced in 1954

—are still so high that they would yield a large surplus of revenues over expenditures if we were at full employment today. They are, in short, repressing demand and incentives in an economy operating well short of its capacity.

To avoid misunderstanding, it is important to stress that any employment program would be unbalanced and incomplete without determined measures (1) to upgrade and adapt the skills and education of the labor force to the more exacting demands of our advancing technology and (2) to facilitate the flow of workers from job to job, industry to industry, and place to place. Nevertheless, our principal reliance for a return to the 4 per cent or better levels of unemployment we took for granted in the early postwar period must be on measures to boost demand for the products of American industry and agriculture.

The amount of the increase in total demand which would be necessary to reduce unemployment to the 4 per cent interim-target level can be approximated in several ways. We have made direct estimates of the relationship between unemployment rates and output levels; and we have independently estimated the potential GNP that the economy could produce at 4 per cent unemployment. . . . Except for small differences reflecting cyclical variations in productivity and erratic fluctuations in labor force participation rates, these estimates of potential output (in constant prices) are very closely approximated by a 3.5 per cent trend line passing through actual GNP in mid-1955. . . .

Our analysis . . . suggests that total demand for goods and services would have had to average some $30 billion higher than it was in each of these past two years for unemployment to average 4 per cent. The basic purpose of the tax cut is to close that $30 billion gap—and to realize the benefits to employment, growth, and our international competitive position that will flow from this advance.

To be sure, by the time the full effects of the proposed two-stage tax cut will be reflected in demand and output, the economy's potential will have grown considerably, and total demand growth will therefore have to be considerably more than $30 billion. But when the tax cut lifts the expanding level of private demand in the U.S. economy by the extra $30 billion (in terms of 1963 GNP and price levels) that can confidently be expected, it will have achieved its basic purpose. Had this increase been effective during the past six years, it would have eliminated our persistent slack and allowed our unemployment rate to average 4 per cent. . . .

THE PERSISTENT PROBLEMS
OF STRUCTURAL UNEMPLOYMENT

The tax cut would thus increase demand to levels consistent with a 4 per cent rate of unemployment. It would ease our most pressing unemployment problems.

Experience (which we will review later in this statement) clearly shows (1) that the unemployment rate will decline for every major category of workers and (2) that the sharpest declines will occur where the incidence of unemployment is the highest: among teen-agers, the Negroes, the less skilled, the blue-collar groups generally.

But even so, the unemployment rates of many groups will still be intolerably high. Back in 1957, for instance, when the average unemployment rate was just over 4 per cent for the whole economy, the rates were much higher for many disadvantaged groups and regions—e.g., 10.8 per cent for teen-agers, 8.0 per cent for nonwhites, 9.4 per cent for unskilled manual workers, and 11.5 per cent for workers in Wilkes-Barre–Hazleton, Pennsylvania.

These *high specific unemployment rates, which persist even when the general rate falls to an acceptable level,* are the essence of the problem of structural unemployment. Even a fully successful tax cut cannot solve problems like these by itself. They require a more direct attack.

To reduce the abnormally high and stubborn unemployment rate for Negroes requires a major improvement in their education and training and an attack on racial discrimination. To reduce the persistent high rate for the unskilled and the uneducated groups demands measures to help them acquire skills and knowledge. To reduce excessive unemployment associated with declining industries and technological advance requires retraining and relocation. To reduce high unemployment in distressed areas of Pennsylvania, Michigan, Minnesota, and elsewhere calls for special measures to rebuild the economic base of those communities and assist their workers.

Both the Administration and the Congress have recognized that these measures must be taken concurrently with measures to expand aggregate demand. Coal miners in Harlan County are structurally unemployed *now*, and so are Negro and Puerto Rican youths in New York City. Yet, programs to reduce structural unemployment will run into severe limits *in the absence of an adequate growth of demand*—i.e., in the absence of rapid expansion of total job opportunities. Such expansion is needed to assure that retrained and upgraded workers, for example, *will* find jobs at the end of the training period and *will not* do so at the expense of job opportunities for other unemployed workers. As structural programs create new and upgraded skills, they will in some cases fit the participants for jobs that had previously gone begging. But for the most part, the needed jobs must be created by expansion of total demand.

Quite apart from the human significance of structural unemployment, it also has great economic importance. For only as we reduce structural and frictional unemployment can we achieve the higher levels of total output which would be associated with unemployment rates below our 4 per cent interim target.

Every worker needlessly unemployed represents a human cost which offends the sensibilities of a civilized society. But each worker needlessly unemployed also represents a waste of potential goods and services, which even an affluent society can ill afford. More intensive measures to attack structural unemployment are necessary to reduce the unemployment rate not merely to 4 per cent, but beyond.

HAS STRUCTURAL UNEMPLOYMENT INCREASED?

The preceding section addressed itself to structural unemployment as a human and social problem and considered its role in the process of lowering the unemployment rate to and below 4 per cent. But it is also appropriate to ask: Has structural unemployment increased to such an extent since 1957—the last time unemployment was near 4 per cent—that it will impede the expansionary effects of demand-creating measures in general and the tax cut in particular?

A reading of the evidence on this score must focus principally on what happens, over time, to the unemployment rates of particular groups—teen-agers, untrained and unskilled workers, Negroes, and other disadvantaged groups and regions—in relation to the total unemployment rate. It would clearly be misleading simply to compare unemployment rates for such groups in a year like 1957, when the total rate was about 4 per cent, with the corresponding rates in 1962-63, when the total rate has averaged 5.6 per cent. Rather, it is the *relationship* between the total rate and the groups' rates—and its historical development—that reveals whether the structural problem is getting worse or not. And this relationship has been remarkably stable.

The disadvantaged groups almost invariably share more than proportionately—and the skilled and white-collar groups less than proportionately—in both decreases and increases in total employment. In the past, when the over-all unemployment rate has risen (or fallen) one percentage point, the rate for nonwhites and teen-agers has risen (or fallen) by about two percentage points, the rate for unskilled workers by about two and one half percentage points. But the rate for professional and technical workers has risen or fallen by only about one fourth of a percentage point.

One obvious reason for the disproportionate impact on teen-agers is that they are the most recent additions to the labor force. When new job opportunities are few, there is a backing-up at the point of entry. Furthermore, even when they do find jobs, they tend to have the lowest seniority and are therefore first to be laid off. Much the same is true of Negroes. Given existing patterns of discrimination, they are often in marginal jobs or at the bottom of seniority lists. Moreover, when jobs are scarce and labor is plentiful, racial discrimination, where it exists, is more likely to enter into hiring and firing decisions. And at such times, employers are also more inclined to pass over inexperienced and untrained workers and less inclined to press their own efforts to adapt such personnel to their needs via in-service training programs. They tend to be less aggressive in seeking new employees outside their own local labor markets. And labor supply considerations are less likely to determine the location of new plants.

On the other hand, employers do not typically discharge many supervisory and technical personnel when output drops and, as a result, they do not need to expand their employment of such persons proportionately when output rises.

Moreover, there are other reasons why the employment of many categories of workers does not rise and fall in the same proportion

as the total. . . . For example, the rate of inventory accumulation is
highly sensitive to the rate of expansion or contraction in total output, and goods that typically are inventoried tend to require large
numbers of production workers. In contrast, the service industries,
whose output is not subject to inventory accumulation nor to such
wide fluctuations in consumption, generally use more technical and
white-collar workers.

Thus it is not surprising to find that slackened demand since 1957
has intensified intergroup and interregional disparities in unemployment rates at the same time that it raised the total unemployment
rate. Nonwhites, teen-agers, unskilled and semiskilled workers have
suffered a greater-than-average increase in unemployment since
1957. But these same groups will also benefit disproportionately as
demand expands and the over-all unemployment rate declines. This
point is illustrated in Table 1, which shows how the incidence of unemployment changed during the 1960-61 recession and the 1961-62
recovery.

Table 1

Change in unemployment rate, selected groups and areas

	Percentage points	
	1960-61	1961-62
Total	1.1	−1.1
Teen-agers	1.6	−1.9
Nonwhites	2.3	−1.5
Nonfarm laborers	2.0	−2.1
Operatives	1.6	−2.1
Manufacturing workers	1.5	−1.9
Miners	2.1	−3.0
For illustrative purposes:		
Michigan	3.4	−3.4
Wheeling, W. Va.	6.9	−7.8

Studies of changes in the incidence of unemployment among unskilled and semiskilled blue-collar workers—whose jobs would seem
to be highly vulnerable to technological change—can provide important insights into the structural unemployment problem. One
would expect an accelerated rate of technological displacement to

be reflected in rising rates of unemployment for these groups—relative to total unemployment. One would also expect to find such a relative rise for workers in industries such as manufacturing, mining, and transportation where automation has so far found its widest application.

To test this possibility, we have correlated the unemployment rate in specific occupations and industries with the rate for all experienced workers in the labor force during the 1948-57 period—in other words, for the period before the main structural unemployment upsurge is alleged to have occurred. These correlations were then used to calculate what the occupational and industrial distribution of unemployment *would* have been in 1962 if the old relationships had held. If there had been a substantial increase in structural maladjustments, the actual 1962 unemployment rates for what we may call the "technologically vulnerable groups" should have been *higher* than these calculated rates. But in fact, as Table 2 shows, a majority of the rates are *lower*. For some of these occupations and industries, the actual increase in unemployment was greater than expected, but in most cases it was less. And taking all of the blue-collar occupations and goods-producing industries together, we also find that the rise in actual unemployment was somewhat less than the 1948-57 experience would have suggested.

We do not conclude from this evidence, nor from similar findings by Edward Denison and Otto Eckstein as to the *geographic* distribution of unemployment, that a reduction in structural unemployment has occurred. Similarly, however, we do not conclude that the unusually high unemployment rates experienced by teen-agers this year, or the rather low rates experienced by adult males, prove an adverse structural shift. In some labor market areas, imbalances have lessened; in others, they have increased. But this does not suggest that the over-all rate of structural unemployment has risen significantly.

The evidence reviewed above does not yield persuasive indications that structural elements are today a significantly larger factor in our unemployment than in 1957. Nevertheless, it would not be surprising if some particular aspects of structural unemployment have intensified. . . . The longer a period of slack persists, the more likely . . . the detailed structure of skills, experience, and training of the labor force would fail to reflect fully . . . job requirements at high

Table 2

Unemployment rates in industries and occupations most vulnerable to
technological displacement, 1957 and 1962
(Per cent)

Industry or occupation	1957	1962	Change in rate, 1957-62	
			Actual	Expected[1]
All workers	4.3	5.6	1.3	...
Experienced wage and salary workers	4.5	5.5	1.0	...
Workers in selected industries (goods-producing)	5.4	6.4	1.0	1.3
Mining, forestry, and fisheries	6.3	8.6	2.3	1.8
Construction	9.8	12.0	2.2	1.8
Durable-goods manufacturing	4.9	5.7	.8	1.4
Nondurable-goods manufacturing	5.3	5.9	.6	1.0
Transportation and public utilities	3.1	3.9	.8	1.0
Experienced workers	3.9	4.9	1.0	...
Workers in selected occupations (blue-collar)	6.0	7.4	1.4	1.7
Craftsmen, foremen, and kindred workers (skilled)	3.8	5.1	1.3	1.3
Operatives and kindred workers (semiskilled)	6.3	7.5	1.2	1.6
Laborers, except farm and mine (unskilled)	9.4	12.4	3.0	2.6

[1] Calculated by use of correlations of (1) unemployment rates by industry with the rate for all experienced wage and salary workers, and (2) unemployment rates by occupation with the rate for all experienced workers, using data for the period 1948-57 in both cases.

Sources: Department of Labor and Council of Economic Advisers.

levels of employment. High employment in 1967 will call for a some-what different pattern of jobs than . . . in 1957, and a slack labor market does not accurately foretell what that pattern will be. More-over, there is danger that, after a long period of slack, new hiring standards, habits of mind, and expectations appropriate to an "easy" labor market will have become entrenched, rationalizing increased discriminations against disadvantaged groups. Thus, after the period of prolonged slack since 1957, there is . . . need . . . to assist demand-stimulating policies in tailoring men to jobs and jobs to men. . . .

It is feared that as demand increases, there will not be enough highly educated workers to fill the key technical and professional positions that must be manned if production is to expand to levels consistent with 4 per cent unemployment; that, in consequence, expansion of output will be frustrated; and that, because of this, high percentages of the remainder of the labor force—including poorly educated workers—will be left unemployed.

It is important to distinguish this quite specific point about near-term bottlenecks from other propositions about the economic importance of education. It is unquestionably true, we believe, that greatly reinforced education is needed to press the attack on the pockets of long-term structural unemployment that have plagued the economy for a long time.

Shifting Educational Requirements

. . . The clearly indicated rise in the requirement for teachers, scientists, physicians, engineers, technicians, and nurses poses obvious demands on education in general and higher education in particular. And increased demands for many special skills create needs for expanded programs of vocational education and for more persons with a basic high school education. . . .

Likewise, there can be little doubt about the enormous importance of education as an engine for stimulating the long-term growth of our productive potential. Edward Denison has estimated that 42 per cent of the increase in output *per worker* between 1929 and 1957 was the result of education and another 36 per cent the result of the general advance in the application of scientific and technological knowledge to which our educational process and institutions clearly were heavy contributors. All of these are extremely important —in fact, conclusive—reasons for strengthening our educational programs.

But they should not be confused with the view that educational deficiencies prevent the solution of our current problem of excessive unemployment, and, specifically, that near-term manpower bottlenecks will significantly restrain a demand expansion—stimulated by a tax cut—from accomplishing its employment objective. The statistical testing of the educational bottleneck hypothesis turns out, if properly done, to be a very complex undertaking. . . . However, some reliable impressions already have emerged from the figures at hand. One is that, while there does appear to have been some rise in the demand for highly educated workers relative to their supply during the postwar period *as a whole,* the timing of this change is crucial for purposes of evaluating the bottleneck thesis. Since the economy operated at approximately a 4 per cent unemployment rate in the mid-1950's without encountering serious skilled-manpower bottlenecks, the key question is whether most of this shift occurred *before* or after the 1955-57 period. Hence a shift in job educational requirements relative to supply that had occurred before those years, and was not serious enough to obstruct expansion then, poses little threat to a new move back toward 4 per cent unemployment now.

The available unemployment data seems to show that whatever shift may have occurred in job educational requirements relative to supply *did* occur prior to 1957. Indeed it may have been partially reversed since that time. From 1957 to 1962, for example, the unemployment rate for male workers with an eighth-grade education or less rose by about one half, roughly the same as the rate of overall unemployment. But the unemployment rate for college graduates rose from 0.6 per cent to 1.4 per cent.

In addition to unemployment rates, the percentages of labor force participation by groups of different educational attainments also have changed during the postwar period. Here the data currently in hand do not permit us to locate the timing of these changes to the degree that has been possible with the unemployment rates. And so we simply do not know whether here, too, the shift toward greater participation by the well-educated, and lesser participation by the poorly educated, may largely have occurred before 1957.*

If, in the absence of information, one assumes that the shift in relative participation rates occurred more recently, one might conclude that there have been some withdrawals from the labor force by

---

* From data examined since the testimony was prepared, it appears that the shift toward greater participation by the well-educated primarily occurred before 1957; as to the poorly educated, roughly half of the shift toward lower participation occurred prior to and half after 1957.

poorly educated male workers. Whenever they occurred, they present an obvious challenge to both public and private training programs. But the magnitude of these shifts is easily exaggerated—especially if one fails to make adequate allowance for the improvements in retirement programs during the past dozen years. It is clear that the vast majority of the so-called "losses" of less educated workers from the male labor force were concentrated in the sixty-five-and-older age group.

. . . The real nub of the issue . . . is the failure of the bottleneck hypothesis to make any allowance for the proven capacity of a free labor market—especially one endowed with a high average level of education and enterprise and expanding programs to improve labor skills and mobility—to reconcile discrepancies between particular labor supplies and particular labor demands.

If relative shortages of particular skills develop, the price system and the market will moderate them, as they always have done in the past. Employers will be prompted to step up their in-service training programs and, as more jobs become available, poorly skilled and poorly educated workers will be more strongly motivated to avail themselves of training, retraining, and adult education opportunities. Government manpower programs begun in the 1961-63 period will also be operating to help ease the adjustment of specific shortages.

The highly-educated-manpower-bottleneck argument arrives at its alarming conclusion by projecting to new situations a perfectly static set of educational requirements. The argument makes no allowance for flexibility in the system. Flexibility, of course, is not unlimited. If we were talking about accomplishing a massive increase in output within a few months, manpower bottlenecks might indeed become critical. But we find it unrealistic to believe that they represent a major constraint upon an extra $30 billion of output in what will soon be a $600 billion economy—especially when (1) there are virtually no current signs of tension in either labor markets or product markets and (2) the demand expansion that will accomplish the closure will be spread over two or more years in which continuing new supplies of highly trained manpower will be entering the labor market.

It is difficult to believe that an economy that was able to absorb the dramatic shifts needed to convert to war production in World

War II, and that operated at unemployment levels as low as 1.2 per
cent during that war and more recently (1953) at 2.9 per cent,
could not move rather readily, over the space of two or three years,
to our interim target of 4 per cent unemployment.

. . . The Europeans have maintained unemployment rates considerably lower than ours. After adjustment for conceptual differences, the unemployment rate in 1960 was 1.0 per cent in Germany,
1.9 per cent in France, and 4.3 per cent in Italy. In Italy and Germany these low rates represented a considerable improvement over
earlier postwar experience, and the higher Italian rate has subse-
quently declined materially.

The major explanation for such low unemployment rates in economies undergoing such profound transitions lies in the maintenance
of a very high level of demand. During the 1950's the average annual growth rate in France was 4 per cent, in Italy, 6 per cent, and
in Germany, over 7 per cent—and both Italy and France have had
even higher rates so far in the 1960's. This experience demonstrates
beyond any doubt that, under the stimulus of adequate demand,
and with the aid of active labor market policies, modern economies
are sufficiently resilient to absorb poorly educated workers, to adapt
to skill shortages, and to adjust to rapid technological change in a
manner which maintains extremely low unemployment rates. This
European experience—which in broad outline has been matched in
Japan—reassures us that, once high and growing demand presses our
capacity, we too will adapt to rapid change and maintain our
economic health.

Structural unemployment is a human and an economic problem
that we must attack by every means available. But the expansion of
total demand through tax reduction remains the crucial central element in our attack upon unemployment.

        ❖   ❖   ❖

The Trend of Labor Productivity

Some recent developments have been cited frequently to support
the belief that technological change is accelerating. In certain instances, automation has greatly lifted output per man-hour and has
revolutionized the productive process. These instances are highly
dramatic, but they are insufficient for evaluating the over-all impact

of technological progress. Such an evaluation must be based on a study of the trend in over-all productivity—output per man-hour—for the private economy.

The main difficulty in assessing the trend of productivity is that current output per man-hour is also affected by numerous transitory factors, most significantly by fluctuations in output and changes in the average age of the machinery in use. For example, during recessions employment falls proportionately less than output as a result of lags in employer reaction, uncertainty about the future, the need to retain the same supervisory and maintenance personnel over wide ranges of output, and hiring and firing costs. Employed manpower is not fully utilized, and the level of output per man-hour is depressed. This is usually followed by rapid rates of increase in labor productivity during the early phases of cyclical expansions.

Moreover, our statistical measures of productivity are far from exact. Recorded changes in productivity for individual years and sectors must be viewed as a broad gauge—rather than a precise reading—of economic performance.

With this qualification, productivity measurements for recent years are presented in Table 3, accompanied by some comparisons with longer-run trends. Labor input data are based on information collected primarily from establishments. The table shows that productivity gains have been healthy but not unprecedentedly large during the past three years. Although improvement has varied among sectors, the average gain in each case has been greater during the past three years than in the preceding decade, but less than the average of 1947-50.

To determine whether these relatively larger gains of the past three years exceed past trends, it is necessary to sort out the cyclical and transitory factors affecting productivity. For this purpose, several alternative statistical analyses were undertaken on the nonfarm productivity gains of 1949-60 to determine the separate influences on productivity of the average age of equipment stocks, variations in the growth of output, and changes in the degree of capacity utilization. These findings were then used to estimate the productivity gains that might have been expected in the years 1961 through 1963 if the past relationships and trends still held.

Depending on which statistical analysis is used (and there is no clear basis for preferring one to another), the recent gains are

Table 3

Changes in output per man-hour in the private economy, 1919-63

			Percentage change per year		
				Nonagriculture	
Period	Total private	Agriculture	Total	Manufac- turing[1]	Nonmanu- facturing[1]
1919-47	2.2	1.4	2.0	[2]3.0	[3]
1947-63	3.2	6.1	2.6	2.7	2.5
1947-50	4.5	8.8	3.7	4.3	3.4
1950-60	2.7	5.4	2.1	2.0	2.2
1960-63	3.5	5.5	3.2	3.7	2.9
1960-61	3.3	5.9	2.9	2.6	3.1
1961-62	3.9	3.4	3.8	5.4	2.9
1962-63	3.5	7.4	3.0	3.1	2.8

[1] Department of Labor estimates for 1960-63 are in the course of revision and are not available. . . . Therefore estimates for all years beginning with 1947 have been made by the Council of Economic Advisers on a consistent basis using Department of Commerce net output estimates.

[2] Based on data from private sources.

[3] Not available.

NOTE: Man-hours are based primarily on establishment data.

Sources: Department of Commerce, Department of Labor, and Council of Economic Advisers.

either about in line with the expectation or exceed it by amounts ranging up to one percentage point. These differences are sufficiently tentative that further experience is needed to confirm a positive conclusion.

Recent large gains could reflect no more than a possibly unusually cautious hiring policy on the part of business in the current expansion. Experience with the slack labor market of recent years may have deterred the anticipatory hiring of overhead and skilled personnel, which appears typically to take place during a business expansion as insurance against the possibility of future labor shortages. If so, the recent higher rates of productivity increase may prove to be transitory. Yet optimism may still be warranted. If objective analysis does not support a firm conclusion that the trend of productivity has accelerated, neither can that possibility be dismissed. Technological progress may indeed have accelerated, but its impact on productivity may be only gradually becoming visible because of the time that must elapse before innovations become embodied in new capital equipment and expressed in new organizational forms.

❋   ❋   ❋

THE CHALLENGE OF AUTOMATION

In a way it is surprising how reluctant we are to embrace the higher productivity levels and living standards which "automation" makes possible. Some of the more popular literature on the subject treats it as a new and frightening development. But in fact, it is only the most recent aspect of a continuing process of technological advance that dates back to the beginning of the Industrial Revolution. Taking full advantage of this process, the United States has built the most productive and most remunerative economy in the world. Through time, brute strength has been progressively replaced by simple machines, mechanical power, complex machines, assembly lines, and today increasingly by sophisticated automatic feedback systems. At each stage of the process individuals were temporarily displaced from existing jobs, new skills were found to be needed and were acquired, and total output and employment expanded as demand increased in line with the new higher production capabilities.

Ultimately the total effect has always in the past been a higher standard of living for almost everyone—higher pay for workers, cheaper and better products for consumers, and larger profits for businessmen and stockholders. On the basis of our historical experience, automation should be recognized for what it is—an open door to a more productive economy, to higher levels of private consumption, to more effective public services, and to larger resources for the support of our international objectives.

Doubts about our ability to adjust to automation seem to be based on two questions: Can we really use the enlarged output of goods and services made possible by a rising rate of productivity advance? Will the new speed and character of technological change create impossible problems of adjustment for the labor force?

Those who raise the first question sometimes argue that we cannot possibly consume all that the new techniques can produce—that the persistent high level of unemployment over the past few years is evidence of "satiation"—that the fantastic productivity of the American economy has outdistanced the needs of the American people. What do the facts show?

First and most obvious, it is impossible to square this notion with the persistence of poverty in the American economy. We are indeed an affluent society, by every comparative standard. Nonetheless, even in this age of affluence, one fifth of American families still have annual incomes below $3,000—that is, they live in poverty. To them, the suggestion that we are economically satiated must seem ridiculous, if not cruel. Until our society has met the challenge of poverty in the midst of plenty, it is in no danger of being satiated with goods and services.

But—quite apart from the persistence of poverty—there is nothing in the economic behavior of even the more affluent American consumers to support the satiation hypothesis. At all income levels—except perhaps in the top 2 or 3 per cent of the income-wealth distribution—the ratio of consumption to disposable income is one of our most stable economic relationships. Year in, year out—ever since 1950—American consumers have continued to spend from 92 to 94 per cent of their . . . income after taxes on consumer goods and services. During this period total income and average family income have both risen markedly; but there is no evidence of any growing disinclination to spend a stable and high percentage of each additional dollar of income on consumption.

This does not, of course, rule out the possibility that—as in the past—some, many, or even all of us will prefer to forego still higher income in favor of greater leisure in the form of shorter hours, longer vacations, or earlier retirements. (There are indications, incidentally, that many people find it easier to become satiated with leisure than with income!)

In addition to unsatisfied private consumption needs, there are pressing needs for goods and services which are ordinarily and, in some cases, inevitably provided by the public sector. Admittedly there is disagreement as to just which of these "public" goods most need to be increased. There are also differences of opinion as to which levels of government should undertake expanded activities. Nevertheless, almost all major segments of the American community support increases in the level of one or another of such

"public" goods and services, whether they be, for example, urban renewal, or improved health services, or better schools, or better roads and airports, or purer water and air, or more adequate facilities in national parks. Certainly none of this bespeaks a satiated society.
. . . The second question raised about our ability to adjust to automation concerns the labor force adjustments it necessitates. If the advance of technological progress has speeded up, it is reasonable to suppose that, as a by-product, the rate at which particular skills are rendered obsolescent is also increasing. But a further and different point is sometimes made: namely, that automation (in its narrower technical sense) is shifting not merely the *rate* but the *character* of skill requirements generated by technological change. Previously, it is suggested, technological change simplified the work process and hence created many semiskilled jobs, which could be filled by workers with little training. Automation, however, reintegrates the production process and thus eliminates many unskilled and semiskilled jobs.

Whether this interpretation is correct is a highly complex empirical question. Many of the jobs displaced by automation are low-skilled and some of the jobs added are extremely high-skilled. The design and installation of automation equipment surely requires highly trained personnel. Yet the need for these people is clearly limited, and they do not stay with the equipment long after installation. Once in operation, the equipment may actually diminish rather than raise skill requirements. Examples of highly automated installations have been cited where all of the maintenance is done by high school graduates with a fairly short trade school course in electronic repair. High skills are required for the programming function, but this also tends to be concentrated in the initial stages and "canned" programs are increasingly available in some applications. A good deal more study and experience is needed before we can safely generalize about the impact of automation on skill requirements for the labor force as a whole.

Beyond the question of how automation (in the narrow sense) affects average skill requirements lies the broader question of the impact on labor markets of any general acceleration that may occur in the rate of technological advance. This broader question involves at least two dimensions.

A "vertical" dimension relates to the impact of speeded technological change on the long-term rate of increase in the average educational content of jobs. As noted repeatedly, our past rapid increase in educational levels has both responded to and helped bring about our steady technological advance and rising productivity. The exact nature of the complex interrelationships between the average educational accomplishment of the labor force, job educational requirements, and a further speeding up of the pace of technological advance is a matter for some speculaion. But whatever the answer, more and better education will continue to have one of the highest priorities among the values of American society.

The "horizontal" dimension of our question requires less speculation. We can be certain that a speeded pace of technological change will increase the rate of job displacement, and will require even greater attention to measures for improving labor mobility, for training and retraining of workers, and for an effective level of basic education to promote adaptability and flexibility. The possibility of an accelerated pace of technical change thus underscores an already powerful case for stronger labor market policies to meet existing problems of displacement.

                               *   *   *

Defects of the Adjustment Process

Displaced workers rarely find new jobs instantaneously. Time is required for the flow of job information and for matching the location, education, skill, wage, working conditions, and other preferences of job-hunters with the requirements of employers. Personal contacts, employment services, and "help wanted" advertisements provide important channels of communication between employers hunting for workers, and workers hunting for jobs. Nonetheless, the flow of labor market information is unnecessarily slow and circumscribed. Because of insufficient staff and, in some instances, because of the failure of employers to provide information, local offices of the Federal-State Employment Service cannot provide complete information on local job opportunities, to say nothing of a full exchange of information among different localities. In the absence of adequate vocational guidance, many young workers are not properly prepared for the activities in which employment is expanding most rapidly. Geographic movement is often restrained by lack of information and by the inability of workers to finance transportation, job search, and change of residence. Occupational mobility is often inhibited by the absence of adequate educational background and the inability to acquire needed skills.

The average displaced worker spends far too long between jobs, even in periods of adequate demand. The average duration of unemployment was 11.6 weeks during the period 1955-57, when the overall unemployment rate averaged 4.3 per cent. And, during the boom years of 1951-53, when the unemployment rate averaged 3.1 per cent and the number of unfilled jobs very probably exceeded the number of unemployed workers, the average duration of unemployment was still 8.7 weeks. These statistics do not refer specifically to the average period of joblessness for workers displaced by technological change, but they do indicate the time-consuming nature of the job-hunting process. They also suggest that reduction of the human cost of technological change will require policies—both private and public—for improving and speeding the matching of available jobs and workers.

Such policies can never be completely adequate. The burdens of transitional unemployment may be harsh, but they sometimes represent only part of the cost of change to the displaced worker. The worker made permanently unemployable by technological change is relatively rare, but it is frequent for a displaced worker to find himself required to accept a less challenging and lower paying job. The specialized skill, experience, and seniority which contributed to earning power in the original job frequently do not have transferable market value.

Moreover, the burden of technological displacement often falls most heavily on those least able to bear it. As noted already, the general drift of technological change has tended to be toward increased rather than reduced skill and education requirements and thus in favor of groups already higher up on the income ladder. To be sure, some of the elite of the labor force have suffered—printers and flight engineers, to take two recent examples. But overwhelmingly, the groups displaced have been the less-skilled, less-educated, and therefore poorer members of the labor force. But even if the incidence of technological change were entirely random, the wealthier community, the more prosperous business, the more highly trained and better paid workers have greater adaptability, and greater resources to help them through the period of adaptation.

When technological change displaces considerable numbers of workers in a particular region or occupation, and these workers lack the skills or mobility necessary to find other jobs quickly, their continuing unemployment can well be called "structural." Pockets of such structural unemployment are never absent, and the problems they present for public policy are intensified (and partly concealed) in a generally slack economy with excessive over-all unemployment.

                                *   *   *

CONCLUSIONS

This statement has been long and necessarily complex. But the issues involved are of the highest urgency and significance for the economic future of our nation, and they are far from simple. . . . These are our principal conclusions:

1. Enactment of the major tax reduction program which is now before the Senate is a necessary condition for solution of the problems that concern this Subcommittee. It will directly add $30 billion to total output and create 2 to 3 million extra jobs. Without the continuing lift in total demands for goods and services that the tax program is designed to accomplish, little progress can be expected in reducing and eliminating problems of excessive unemployment for the nation as a whole. Had this lift in demand been effective in the years 1958 through 1963, it would have overcome economic slack; achieved a considerably higher level of output of needed goods and services; maintained unemployment rates comparable with those realized in the years before 1957; and—in the process— reduced or eliminated our budget deficits.

2. Although tax reduction will alleviate, it will not by itself cure, long-standing problems of structural unemployment, of incomplete adaptation of the structure of our labor force to the structure of demand, of regional imbalances, and of consequent hardship, inequity, and inefficiency. The need to attack these problems stems, first, from our concern to alleviate unnecessary human distress. Second, it stems from the desire to convert unproductive and unwanted idleness into productive employment, so that we can in-

crease our output of needed goods and services even beyond the potential output associated with our interim target of a 4 per cent rate of unemployment. And third, if the rate of technological displacement of workers is in the process of accelerating, it will need to be matched by a similar increase in the mobility and adaptability of our labor force.

This Administration has placed high priority upon measures to accelerate our productivity gains—through the stimulation of investment by tax measures, the improvement of technology in lagging sectors of the civilian economy, and in other ways—with the urgent purpose of improving the competitive position of American producers in world markets and of stepping up our long-term growth rate. It has promoted policies designed to realize the benefits of maximum productive efficiency—policies which may require shifts in our resource use and consequent displacement of labor.

It would be irresponsible not to complement these policies with others designed to facilitate the transfer of resources and to ease necessary burdens of adjustment—as, indeed, was done in the "adjustment" provisions of the Trade Expansion Act.

Without attempting to be comprehensive, we can indicate some of the important channels of attack on structural problems:

—improved labor market information services;
—improved guidance and placement services;
—improved programs of apprenticeship;
—strengthened programs to reduce discriminatory hiring and employment practices by race, sex, or national origin;
—expanded and more effective programs of vocational education, general adult education, and retraining;
—basic improvements in the quality of our educational system at all levels;
—measures to enlarge educational opportunities for children of low income families and minority groups;
—programs to assist the geographical movement of workers;
—expanded policies to strengthen the economic base and to speed the economic growth of distressed communities and regions.

The tax cut and other measures to expand total demand are no substitute for policies like these; while these policies, in turn, are no substitute for a tax cut. Yet a more vigorous expansion of demand will release forces that will powerfully aid in the solution of structural problems. The existence of a stronger demand for labor will by itself strengthen the incentives for workers to undertake training or retraining and for employers to help provide it; will attract workers to move to the places where jobs are plentiful and stimulate employers to assist such movement; will ease the financial burdens on local communities in undertaking improvements in their educational systems; will reduce discriminatory practices both by employers and by unions; and will increase the effectiveness of the free-market price system in encouraging appropriate adjustments of both labor supply and labor demand, the need for which is now partly obscured by slack markets.

3. Important as is the attack on structural problems, we need not fear that structural obstacles will block a healthy expansion of jobs and output resulting from the tax cut. The feasibility of our 4 per cent interim target assumes not some newly perfected system of labor market adjustment but the labor market as it exists today with its present adjustment mechanism. Possible and desirable improvements in our labor market adjustment processes can smooth and accelerate achievement of the interim target. And they can permit us to penetrate beyond it to even lower unemployment rates. But it is on demand stimulus that we must rely to get to the provisional 4 per cent objective.

4. There are hopeful hints in the most recent evidence that we may be achieving a somewhat higher rate of average productivity growth than in the past, although it is too early to be sure. If our potential output per worker should grow more rapidly in the future than in the past, it would mean that an even more rapid expansion of total demand would be required to reach and maintain reasonably full employment of the labor force. But we see no basis for fears that our wants and needs are already satiated, or that total spending will fail to rise with potential output and thus thwart faster expansion. It is true that demand does not *automatically* adjust, year by year, to the growth of potential output. But there is no reason to suppose that demand is more likely to be deficient when potential output is more rapidly growing, than when growth in potential output is less dynamic. On the contrary, the conditions that are conducive to faster productivity growth are also conducive to more rapid expansion in private demands.

Instead of fearing an accelerated growth of productivity, we should and do seek it

—to achieve more fully our private and public domestic economic goals;

—to help us correct our balance-of-payments deficit;

—and to raise the standard and quality of life for all of our citizens.

WHY DO WE HAVE AN UNEMPLOYMENT PROBLEM?

Yale Brozen

Yale Brozen is Professor of Business Economics, Graduate School of Business, University of Chicago. With a background in chemical engineering and economics, he has been Director of Research at Northwestern University's Transportation Center; has taught in Brazil as well as in various U.S. universities; and has written widely on subjects from technology to foreign trade.

We can look for the causes of unemployment in two main areas: (1) external factors acting on the economy; (2) inadequate adaptations of prices and wage rates to offset external factors. External factors include monetary policy, technological change, shifts in consumer tastes, changes in the tax structure, and weather. If prices and wage rates adjust rapidly enough, none of these forces create unemployment. An increase in a payroll tax, for example, causes unemployment only if wage rates fail to fall (or rise less than they would have risen) by the amount of the tax.

Sufficient flexibility in prices and wage rates can *prevent* unemployment in the face of adverse conditions. We must also recognize that prices and wage rates may be moved to levels which *cause* unemployment despite other conditions favoring increased employment. Measures such as the National Industrial Recovery Act and the Agricultural Adjustment Act of 1933 increased wage rates and prices and consequently increased unemployment from 9 million at the time they began operating (September 1933) to 12 million a few months later (January 1934). This occurred when other fac-

From *Employment and Unemployment, The Problem of the 1960's* (Washington, D.C.: Chamber of Commerce of the United States, 1961). Used by permission of the author and the Chamber of Commerce of the United States.

tors would have decreased the number of jobless but for these actions.

Minimum wage laws have decreased the employment of the unskilled, minority groups, and people in disadvantaged areas of the country such as southeast United States and western Pennsylvania. After the Fair Labor Standards Act came into operation in October 1938, for example, and successive increases in the minimum wage rates were imposed in the following years, employment dropped in the seamless hosiery industry in western Pennsylvania, where many plants had been paying less than the minimum rate provided in the Act. The drop occurred during a period of rising employment in the United States.

Studies by John M. Peterson of the University of Arkansas and Marshall Colberg of Florida State University[1] show that increases in minimum wage rates in 1950 and 1956 were responsible for loss of employment opportunities for many people. In large southern pine sawmills Peterson found, from surveys made before and after the imposition of the seventy-five-cent minimum in January 1950, that 17 per cent of the workers in mills averaging below seventy cents per hour lost their jobs. Colberg found similar consequences in low-wage Florida counties stemming from the 1956 increase in minimum wage requirements. Data on unemployment in the whole of the United States in 1956 show a rise in jobless workers under nineteen and unemployed females over forty-five despite an increase in total employment of all workers by 1.8 million in 1956 over the levels prevailing in 1955. These are the workers who bore the brunt of the unemployment created by the 1956 increase in minimum wage levels.

Unions sometimes win wage increases which lift employment costs to levels exceeding those that would prevail in free markets. In these cases, a loss of employment opportunities occurs in the affected industries. Where these industries employ a large proportion of the people of an area, *depressed areas conditions result*. West Virginia suffers from the excessive wage costs imposed by the United Mine Workers. Michigan suffers from the unduly high wage rates set in negotiations between auto manufacturers and the United Auto Workers. Northern Indiana's depression is as much a consequence of the success of the United Steel Workers as it is of the decreased demand for steel.

The relationship between wage rates and job opportunities, given any level of output, has been measured by the group working on regional economics at the University of Chicago under the direction of Dr. Stephen Sobotka. They have found, for example, that a 1 per cent increase in wage rates in the primary metal industry causes approximately a 1.2 per cent decrease in employment in the industry assuming no change in the output of metal.[2] The increased employment costs lead companies to invest in improvement of organization and flow of work, to increase supervision, and to invest in equipment to increase productivity. For a state such as Michigan, given its complex of industries, a 1 per cent increase in manufacturing wage rates decreases job opportunities in Michigan manufacturing by approximately 1.6 per cent, assuming no change in the total manufacturing output of the state. (Of course, increased costs tend to decrease total output and further decrease job opportunities.) . . .

MONETARY CHANGES AND UNEMPLOYMENT

Among the external forces acting on the economy, monetary policy is the major one capable of creating widespread joblessness. Adaptive reactions in the economy adequately cope with most of the other forces when monetary policy does not interfere.[*] Generally, unemployment caused by the variables other than money may be expected to hover around 3 million, or approximately 4 to 5 per cent of the work force.[3] In the case of changes in monetary

---

[*] The adaptive reactions cope with the situation only in the sense of meeting the unemployment problem. When the wage rates of mine workers rise to levels which force coal miners out of jobs, they can generally find other jobs, in the area or by migrating, although usually at lower wage rates, provided normal prosperity prevails. However, union and employer agreement on wage rates which restrict employment opportunities in an industry very frequently forces people out of high-productivity jobs into low-productivity occupations. Also, this prevents people from moving from low-productivity-low-wage jobs to high-productivity jobs. Minimum-wage laws have a similar effect in forcing people out of high-productivity covered occupations into low-productivity, noncovered alternatives. To this extent, *growth in average productivity is slowed* to less than that of which the economy is capable. Since one fourth of the annual productivity gains of the past have come from the shift from low- to high-productivity jobs, wage-setting of the type which prevents this and encourages a reverse movement is indeed pernicious. The adaptive mechanism of the economy does not cope with this problem.

policy, however, we find that adaptations in prices and, particularly, wage rates lag changes in the monetary sphere. As a matter of fact, wage rates seem to move adversely at the very time that monetary forces also behave adversely. Both tend to act together to compound the unemployment problem.

Research by members of the Workshop in Money and Banking at the University of Chicago suggests that turning points in the rate of change in the money supply precede turning points in business activity[4] and in velocity of circulation.* Stability in the money supply growth rate would lead to greater stability in velocity. The combined stability of these two items, which determine the rate of spending, would lead to greater stability in the economy.

The Federal Reserve Board has an unofficial rule of thumb that the money supply should be allowed to grow about 2 per cent per year. The rule, however, is erratically observed. Following the March 1951 accord which freed the Federal Reserve from domination by the Treasury, the Federal Reserve was able to do the excellent job of preventing inflation for which it can be praised. It has, however, done a poor job of stabilizing employment or economic activity. From mid-1951 to mid-1952, it allowed the money supply to grow by 5.6 per cent. In the following year it decreased the rate of growth to 2.5 per cent with a further decrease to 0.8 per cent in 1953-54, thus setting the stage for the rise in unemployment from 1.6 million in 1953 to 3.2 million in 1954. If it had held the rise in money stock under 4 per cent from mid-1951 to mid-1952 (approximately the same rate of growth as that in the preceding year), it would not have had to slow the rate of rise as drastically from 1952 to 1954 to prevent inflation, and the growth in unemployment would have been far more modest.

In early 1958, worried by unemployment and the decline in economic activity, the Board took steps to increase the money stock. It cut required reserve ratios early in the year. From mid-1958 to mid-1959, then, the money stock grew by 3.8 per cent. Once again, the Board allowed the money stock to grow too rapidly.[5] Determined to avoid the 1956 pattern of a rise in prices resulting from its 1954 action, the Board tightened money policy much sooner in the

---

* After a decrease in the rate of increase in the money stock, velocity continues to increase in the lag period before it turns. Similarly, after an increase in the rate of growth of money, velocity declines in the lag period before it turns.

recovery phase than it had before. The result was a pinching off
of the recovery in early 1960 before unemployment had dropped
back to the 1957 level. The growth in money stock was not only
slowed this time; the money stock was actually decreased by 2.1
per cent from mid-1959 to mid-1960. This precipitated the recession
in which we have been in recent months. Once again, the Board
had made the mistake of increasing the stock of money at a greater
than 3 per cent rate. And again, the Board tried to offset the mistake by slowing the growth in stock to much less than 3 per cent.
By slowing the growth in money stock, it again brought about a
recession.

The 3 per cent rate has no magic about it. The required action
for minimizing fluctuations in unemployment is *maintenance of a
steady rate of change in the money stock rather than imposing a
fluctuating rate on the economy.* A steady rate of 1 or 2 per cent
a year is probably as good for the economy—or maybe better—
than a steady 3 per cent rate. A rate fluctuating from 5.6 per cent
to −2.1 per cent (as it did in the decade of the 1950's) is worse
than no change in the stock of money. Without a steady rate of
change, businessmen and labor leaders cannot foresee the consequences of setting any given price for labor. If they gear their
expectations to the past change in money stock, price levels, and
economic activity, the prices they set will turn out to be incompatible
with full employment if the rate of change in money stock is decreased.

Monetary action has caused the deflations of the past which ini-
tiated employment declines. . . . The decrease in the quantity of
money by 16 per cent in 1920 was the direct result of Federal
Reserve policy, beginning with the actions of November 1919. Further steps were taken up to the middle of 1920 to squeeze the
economy[6] in spite of the fact that a downturn in economic activity
began in January 1920.

The 1929-33 decline came from a mixture of causes with monetary
authorities contributing a full measure to the deflation of the quantity of money by 27 per cent. The 1937 descent into depression
was preceded by increases in required reserve ratios in August
1936, and in March and again in May 1937. As a result, the quantity
of money declined continuously throughout 1937 and the first four

months of 1938. The turning point did not come until reserve requirements were reduced in April 1938.

In the postwar period, each of the recessions was preceded by actions on the part of monetary authorities which reduced the rate of growth or decreased the supply of money. The drop in employment which began in late 1948 was preceded by increases in required reserve ratios in February, again in June, and once again in September. These increases forced a decline in the quality of money. The 1953-54 recession was preceded by a period of monetary stringency which was strongest in May 1953. This recession, however, was as much a consequence of the rapid increase in real wage rates between the third quarter of 1952 and the third quarter of 1953 as of monetary policy.

REAL WAGE RATES, PRODUCTIVITY, AND EMPLOYMENT

We can plausibly argue that the unemployment we now suffer, and have suffered, is a consequence of administered prices and wage rates, *given* the monetary circumstances described above. Some of these prices are administered by governmental authorities; others by private authorities.

Many wage rates are set by governmental authorities. Minimum rates for employees of enterprises in interstate commerce have been set by Congress. Much higher minimums have been set for companies producing goods under contract with the United States government by the Secretary of Labor under the powers granted by the Walsh-Healy Act and the Davis-Bacon Act. Other rates are set for long periods in advance by negotiations between employers and unions. On 1961, for example, several million workers in the United States . . . received . . . wage increases under contracts negotiated in prior years when 1961 economic circumstances and markets were but imperfectly known.

The relationship between wage rates and unemployment is such that these 1961 changes . . . add to the number of unemployed, at least in the sense that more people . . . remain unemployed than would have if no wage rate increases occurred. They partially offset the employment-increasing effects of present fiscal and monetary policies, some of which have automatically[7] come into operation, while others are the result of discretionary actions by Congress or by the Federal Reserve Board.

This is not the place to attempt a proof of the proposition that other things being equal, the number of jobs is inversely related to the wage rate. I would like to point to data which illustrate the point that increases in real wage rates which outrun increases in productivity are *frequently* associated with an *increased* volume of unemployment (see Table 1). Purchasing power is determined by factors other than money wage rates.

Between 1929 and 1933, real wage rates in manufacturing rose relative to average output per man-hour by 7 per cent. This was associated with a rise in unemployment in the United States from 1.6 million to 12.8 million. Between 1937 and 1938, real wage rates rose 0.4 per cent more than productivity, and unemployment averaged 10.4 million in 1938 (among those who would have normally been a part of the labor force, unemployment was 9.8 million).[8]

In the various post-World War II recessions, we find similar experiences. The rise in real wage rates outran the average output rise between 1948 and 1949 by almost 2 per cent, and unemployment rose by 1.3 million. From 1952 to 1954, real wage rates again rose almost 2 per cent more than productivity, and unemployment rose by 1.5 million. Between 1956 and 1958, the rise in real wage rates was 0.8 per cent greater than the average output rise, and unemployment rose by 1.7 million. On the other hand, real wage rates rose less than output per man-hour from 1949 to 1950 and 1951. Unemployment declined in these years. Similar experiences have occurred in other years (see Table 2).

I should warn you that average output is not a proper measure of the level of wage rates compatible with full employment. We should use marginal productivity of the total labor force. If average output were highly correlated with marginal productivity, changes in the average would be a guide to changes in marginal output and, therefore, a guide to changes in wage rates consonant with the maintenance of employment. This has been implicitly assumed as true over short periods in the preceding discussion.

Over long periods, we would expect that increases in average output per man caused by a rising supply of capital would be less than changes in marginal output. We would, therefore, expect wage

Table 1

Movement of productivity, wage rates, and unemployment
(in periods of rising unemployment)

Year	Per cent change in real hourly earnings in manufactures[1]	Per cent change in average productivity[2] (private nonfarm sector)	Crude per cent change in productivity relative to wage rate	Unemployment[3] (millions of persons)
1920				1.7
21	+4.1%	−1.1%	−5.2%	5.0
1923				1.4
24	4.5	+3.5	−1.0	2.4
1926				0.9
28	5.8	−0.4	−6.2	2.1
1929				1.6
33	3.6	−3.5	−7.1	12.8
1937				7.7
38	2.4	+2.0	−0.4	10.4
1948				2.1
49	4.8	3.0	−1.8	3.4
1952				1.7
54	7.1	5.4	−1.7	3.2
1956				2.6
58	1.5	0.7	−0.8	4.3

[1] Computed with data from *The Economic Almanac; 1958* (New York: Thomas Y. Crowell Company, 1958), p. 253, and *Economic Indicators* (March 1959).

[2] U.S. Congress, Joint Economic Committee, *Potential Growth of the United States During the Next Decade* (Washington, D.C.: USGPO, 1954), p. 34, for pre-World War II data; *Recent Changes in Output Per Man-Hour* (Washington, D.C.: Bureau of Labor Statistics, January 1959), mimeographed, for postwar data. Bureau of Census series used.

[3] *Historical Statistics of the United States* (Washington, D.C.: USGPO, 1960), p. 73, and *Economic Report of the President* (Washington, D.C.: USGPO, 1961), p. 146. Data from 1957 to date adjusted to maintain comparability with preceding years. No adjustment was made for the change in sampling procedure instituted in 1954. Allowing for this change, unemployment figures for 1954, 1956, and 1958 would be 2.5, 2.0, and 3.3, assuming the same effect proportionately of sample changes in 1956 and 1958 as in 1954.

Table 2

Movement of productivity, wage rates, and unemployment
(in periods of declining unemployment)

Year	Per cent change in real hourly earnings in manufactures[1]	Per cent change in average productivity[2] (private nonfarm sector)	Crude per cent change in productivity relative to wage rate	Unemployment[3] (millions of persons)
1921				5.0
23	+6.2%	+12.01%	+5.8%	1.4
1924				2.4
26	−3.1	5.7	8.8	0.9
1928				2.1
29	+0.7	0.7	0.0	1.6
1933				12.8
36	17.2	19.5	2.3	9.0
1938				10.4
40	6.2	7.6	1.4	8.1
1949				3.4
53	12.4	16.2	3.8	1.6
1954				3.2
55	4.2	4.7	0.5	2.7
1958				4.3
59	3.3	4.2	0.9	3.5

[1] Computed with data from *The Economic Almanac, 1958* (New York: Thomas Y. Crowell Company, 1958), p. 253, and *Economic Indicators* (March 1960).

[2] U.S. Congress, Joint Economic Committee, *Potential Economic Growth of the United States During the Next Decade* (Washington, D.C.: USGPO, 1954), p. 34; *Recent Changes in Output Per Man-Hour* (Washington, D.C.: Bureau of Labor Statistics, January 1959) for data after World War II except change from 1958 to 1959. Data for latter change from *Output Per Man-Hour in the Private Economy* (Washington, D.C.: Bureau of Labor Statistics, June 28, 1960).

[3] *Historical Statistics of the United States* (Washington, D.C.: USGPO, 1960), p. 73, and *Economic Report of the President* (Washington, D.C.: USGPO, 1961), p. 146. Data from 1957 to date adjusted to maintain comparability with preceding years. No adjustment was made for the change in sampling procedure instituted in 1954. Allowing for this change, unemployment figures for 1954, 1955, 1958, and 1959 comparable with preceding years would be 2.5, 2.1, 3.3, and 2.7.

rates to rise by a larger proportion than average output over long periods if an increased supply of capital and capital saving technological change were the dominant forces at work. In fact, we do find that real wage rates rose by nearly 120 per cent between 1929 and 1956, while average output rose by only 93 per cent. Yet 1956 was as good a year in the employment sense as 1929. Changes in average output over long periods are a poor guide to the proper amount of change in wage rates, but may serve well for determination of changes over short periods.

Although the current fashion blames unemployment on automation and structural changes in the economy, I would argue that the unemployment levels of recent months are a consequence of other forces. Automation is in part a response to high wage costs (properly, employment costs including fringe benefits). The automobile and coal mining industries find it necessary to automate and reduce their labor force because wage rates have been set above the levels compatible with productive use of the available manpower. They have been forced to concentrate more capital—more equipment— on fewer men to make them productive enough to be worth employing at current wage levels.

If automatic techniques had not been available, unemployment would be much greater than it now is in these industries. Without automatic techniques, the task of increasing productivity sufficiently to make a man worth employing would have required the concentration of the available capital on even fewer men. More men would have, then, lost their jobs as a consequence of the increases in employment costs which have occurred.

As far as structural changes are concerned, these are again largely the consequence of high wage costs whose incidence has fallen on industries with concentration in certain geographic areas (automobiles in Michigan, coal mining in West Virginia) and on groups with certain types of skills (or lack of skills). Young workers just entering the labor force and older workers lacking skills find their job opportunities narrowed by minimum wage rates set by law or by union-employer agreements. Limits on the number of apprentices agreed upon by unions and employers further frustrate new entrants to the labor market by preventing them from acquiring the skills which would make them worth employing at or above the minimum wage rates.

I would further argue that the unemployment level is higher than it would be with wage levels and prices unchanged—i.e., with the same real wage rates we now have—if the stock of money had not been decreased between 1959 and 1960. . . . With the same level of real wage rates, but a larger stock of money relative to the level of money wage rates and money prices, a larger volume of employment would be provided. Inasmuch as the Federal Reserve Board has been increasing the stock of money since mid-1960, employment levels have finally begun to rise in spite of continuing increases in money wage rates. Employment would rise even faster if the level of money wage rates were increasing less rapidly.

NOTES

1. John M. Peterson, "Employment Effects of Minimum Wages, 1938-50," *Journal of Political Economy* (October 1957).
2. Stephen P. Sobotka, "Michigan's Employment Problem: The Substitution Against Labor," *Journal of Business* (April 1961).
3. For a discussion of the amount of unemployment resulting from technological change, see Y. Brozen, "Automation: Creator or Destroyer of Jobs," *Iowa Business Digest*, 27:2 (February 1956).
4. Clark Warburton's work has also demonstrated this point, although he relates the quantity of money to departures from trend, rather than examining rates of change. "The Misplaced Emphasis in Contemporary Business Fluctuation Theory," *The Journal of the University of Chicago*, 19:4 (October 1946).
5. The rate of growth itself is not as important as the increase from a 0.2 per cent rate to a 3.8 per cent rate.
6. Robert F. Wallace analyzed the especially onerous effect of Federal Reserve policy on agriculture in "The Use of the Progressive Discount Rate by the Federal Reserve System," *Journal of Political Economy*, 64:1 (February 1956).
7. M. Friedman, "Why the American Economy is Depression-Proof," *National-ekonomiska Förenimgens*, 28 (April 1954), describes some of the automatic stabilizers referred to here.
8. From 1936 to 1938, real wage rates rose by 10.9 per cent and average output by 4 per cent. Relative to average output, real wage rates rose by 6.9 per cent. Because of lags, the unemployment effects did not appear until 1938. The measurement and discussion of these lags is beyond the scope of this paper.

INDUSTRIAL STRUCTURE AND GROWTH POTENTIAL

Edgar M. Hoover

Edgar M. Hoover has published major studies on location theory, an enduring interest which he had applied astutely to problems from the development of India to that of New York City. He has taught at Harvard and Michigan and has also served with the National Resources Planning Board, the Central Employment Agency and the Central Intelligence Agency. At present, he is Professor of Economics at the University of Pittsburgh. This article is based on a lecture delivered in Poland and published in the Przeglad Geograficzny.

Regional economic growth is not a smooth, straightforward process. The persistence of efforts to formulate theories of stages of development attests to the existence of important discontinuities. We do not by any means know what all these are, how to foresee them, or how to deal with them. But we do know that the course of development of a region, like that of a nation, encounters from time to time crucial situations in which the future course hangs in the balance and can be influenced by some really major planning decisions. A forking of alternative paths appears. One of the alternatives may be a further growth, along a new line, and the other may be stagnation, sinking into a trap of arrested development or even regression.

These crucial situations present of course the biggest challenge to our insight into the growth-determining factors involved. The stakes

From an address delivered in Poland and published, in Polish, in *Przeglad Geograficzny.* Used by permission of the author.

are highest and the rewards for correct decisions, in terms of economic progress, are at a maximum in such conjunctures.

We are all most familiar from the literature, of course, with the case of so-called underdeveloped nations poised on the threshold of industrialization and threatened by a genuine Malthusian peril of overpopulation. Much effort has gone into defining the conditions necessary for a successful surmounting of the threshold, or the so-called takeoff into a self-sustaining growth process.

But there is also another most important crucial stage, which is my concern in this paper: the situation of the mature industrialized urban region threatened by stagnation. The Pittsburgh region, which a group of us have been intensively studying for the past three or four years, is a perfect example. The rate of growth has been more and more subnormal for many decades. Unemployment is high and chronic. Emigration is heavy. The area appears to have somehow lost the dynamic growth character that brought it to its present importance. . . . There is a feeling that unless something really decisive happens, stagnation will go on indefinitely.

Such a situation can of course arise in a region whose economy is based heavily on a few industries which have themselves ceased to grow or begun to decline. They are the industries of yesterday and today, but not those of tomorrow. But arrested growth in a region may also mean simply that the factors of interregional competition have, in specific industries, taken a trend adverse to that particular region. The region's difficulties are compounded if both of the above conditions apply, so that it finds itself with shrinking shares of shrinking industries.

But in diagnosing the ills of such a "sick" region it is not enough simply to find out the extent to which it is growing relatively slowly in the industries it has, or the extent to which the industries it has are predominantly of types no longer in their fast-growth phase. After all, we could hardly expect that every industry would continue to grow forever, or that any given region could forever retain or increase its relative position in its principal industries. A healthy regional economy can absorb the inevitable losses and shift its resources into new fields, getting its share of the emerging new fast-growth industries to offset the inevitable decline of other activities. When a region fails to make such adjustment successfully, we must ask: "Why?" Perhaps it is simply because the degree of specialization in nongrowing industries was so intense. Perhaps it is because the loss of competitive advantage in some important industries has been so drastic. Or—and here is a possibility I want to emphasize—perhaps it is because the region has developed a sort of economic arthritis that inhibits its ability to adjust to rapidly changing conditions. . . .

Let me explore this question in the context of Pittsburgh, because it is an area I know something about.

A wide variety of industries developed at Pittsburgh early in the nineteenth century, simply by virtue of the city's geographical position as the gateway and outfitting point to the West. It was much later that a big further stimulus to growth came from the other natural advantage that Pittsburgh had—its unrivaled coal resources. Coke was, in fact, not used for making iron in Pittsburgh until 1860, when the city was already a century old.

Pittsburgh became the world's greatest iron and steel center in the latter nineteenth century on the basis of its combined advantage in transportation and fuel supply. At the same time it developed into a leading center of production in glass, machinery, and heavy metal products generally, and built up an accumulation of financial resources and industrial skills and enterprise which encouraged some other industries as well. In two large new industries of the late nineteenth century—aluminum and the manufacture of electrical equipment—Pittsburgh was a leader from the start: partly by historical accident but also partly by virtue of the investment capital and business enterprise accumulated in the older industries. The fact that two new fuels—petroleum and natural gas—were first commercially exploited in western Pennsylvania made some further contribution to Pittsburgh's growth in that period. For example, the steel mills of Pittsburgh still command a large share of the market for pipe and other steel products used in the petroleum industry, despite the fact that the bulk of American petroleum production and refining is now in other areas, mostly far distant from Pittsburgh.

For a number of reasons, Pittsburgh failed to maintain its competitive advantage in any of its principal specialties. This was inevitable in view of developments in transportation trade and regional development that reduced the strategic value of Pittsburgh's gateway position at the source of the Ohio River. It was inevitable in view of technological developments that reduced the locational importance of the special types of coking coal of the Pittsburgh region for the steel industry. It was inevitable in view of the gradual industrialization of the whole area to the west and the rise of numerous industrial competitors at least as well situated as Pittsburgh to serve the new industrial markets of the interior.

Historically it appears that these adverse developments, combined with a slackening in the national rates of growth of employment in some of the industries involved, hit the Pittsburgh economy particularly hard in the period beginning about 1920. It is during the past forty to fifty years that this region has definitely lagged behind national trends and has shown unmistakable symptoms of chronic economic debility. This is true despite the fact that substantial further growth has occurred in population, in overall and per capita real income, and in the physical volume of output in many important industries including steel.

The symptoms, which have tended to increase gradually in their gravity, have included, for example, a net outward migration of people from the metropolitan region as a whole. In each decade since the 1920's, the net outflow has been greater than in the previous decade. This is quite exceptional among American metropolitan regions, most of which have continued to attract a net inflow of migrants from nonmetropolitan areas. Absolute declines in employment have occurred particularly in coal mining, where the region now employs only about one eighth as many miners as it did at the peak (some fifty years ago). That trend reflects in part the very rapid increase in output per man-hour that has characterized the American coal mining industry in general and the rather stagnant trend of total national coal output in recent decades; but it also reflects in part a steadily diminishing share of the Pittsburgh region in the coal mining industry of the nation. Employment in the region in steel, electrical machinery, glass, and metal fabricating industries has not shown similar drastic or longstanding declines but, in the period since the last world war, has followed horizontal or—in some cases—apparently declining trends. And finally, the area has not developed any significant position in such young and growing manufacturing industries as electronics, the manufacture of household appliances, synthetic fibers, automobiles, aircraft, or the more highly processed chemicals. . . .

Historical changes in the pattern of transport costs and in the distribution of major markets, and technological changes affecting materials requirements and the economics of scale and integration of operations, tell the story of the Pittsburgh region's changing competitive position in such industries as coal and coke, iron and steel, chemicals, glass, and heavy metal fabricating and machinery industries.

Thus, for example, the area's original position of almost unique advantage in iron and steel production had been undermined partly by changes in technology. These had, first, the effect of reducing the weight of materials inputs relative to output, or the Weberian material index of the process. Less and less coal has been required per ton of coke, and less and less coke (as well as somewhat less iron ore) per ton of iron produced. At the same time, technical improvements in both coke ovens and blast furnaces made it possible to utilize a wider range of qualities of coal for metallurgical purposes. Not only have materials inputs lessened in relative quantity, but regional differentials in cost of materials have very much narrowed, so that today there is very little difference in overall materials assembly costs among the steelmaking locations of the eastern and central United States. That development has virtually removed one of the main bases of Pittsburgh's primacy. Proximity to markets has become more and more important for the location of steelmaking, and more and more of the other regions of the country have developed large enough markets to support their own iron and steel metalworking complexes.

In relation to the present pattern of markets and of competing production centers, the Pittsburgh area's steel industry is still somewhat overgrown. To dispose of more than a minor fraction of its capacity output, it has to ship into markets which are closer to some other producing center. In general, the Pittsburgh mills must absorb substantial amounts of transport charges to compete in those markets, and this, of course, cuts into profit margins. Our study was able to arrive at at least a rough quantitative measure of this market handicap by analyzing data on the location of steel markets and the transportation costs to each of those markets from each producing center. A further trend toward generally closer correspondence between each region's capacity and the fraction of the national market with respect to which it is advantageously located would inevitably call for some further scaling down of the Pittsburgh region's fractional share of national steel output, which is roughly one seventh. No one expects this to happen very quickly, however, since in the absence of quite revolutionary changes in technology the industry displays great locational inertia for generally sound economic reasons. By getting into the lead in plant modernization, as some Pittsburgh firms have done, the area appears to have a good chance to continue to increase its level of steel output. It does not, however, seem to have any prospect of fully keeping pace with the growth of the steel industry in the rest of the country. And in view of the very rapid labor-saving advances being made and in prospect in the industry, there is every reason to expect that the region's employment in the steel industry will fall off markedly in the foreseeable future.

In coal mining, a partially different set of market and technical changes explain the Pittsburgh region's decline in relative importance and a steady decline in employment of miners over the past forty years. The once extremely important advantage of the special coking qualities of some of the region's coal has become far less important. The iron and steel industry, a major factor in the market, has dispersed into other areas, which have alternative fuel sources. The rise of petroleum fuels has wholly taken away from coal such industrial markets as the glass industry, plus the transportation market (railroads and waterways), plus the domestic space-heating market. The big growth market for coal now is the electric-power industry; and although this and some other developments are expected to start the national trend of coal consumption rising again, the mines of the Pittsburgh region are not in a unique position to profit thereby. Some tendency toward competitive disadvantage arising from depletion of the most accessible coal deposits is evident in many parts of the region, where coal has been mined continuously for two hundred years. In coal as in steel, regional output may increase somewhat; but, because of continued progress in labor-saving improvements, employment can be expected to drop still further. . . .

. . . In glass, a field in which Pittsburgh was at one time by far the most important producing center in the country, the fuel has been natural gas rather than coal since the 1880's. This region's supplies of natural gas, though continuing to be a valuable resource, now appear small in relation to those of other areas, as the South-west's, and fall far short of meeting local demand. The major glass markets are the automobile, furniture, and construction indus-tries, and none of those is significantly concentrated in or near the region.

Again, in the making of transportation equipment, the Pittsburgh region's almost exclusive specialty has been railroad equipment, the market for which has declined while the automobile and aircraft production industries have sought other locations. The textile and apparel industries have virtually disappeared from the region, since it does not possess either of the key advantages of exceedingly cheap labor or quick contact with such fashion garment centers as New York. The aluminum industry, which originated in Pittsburgh, has dispersed to locations where electric power is still cheaper.

The biggest question of all, however, and certainly the most im-portant for the region's future, is why the regional economy has not shown more resilience in adapting to change. As its traditional industrial mainstays have weakened, why have not enough new industries appeared to take up the slack? Is Pittsburgh inherently a poor location for any industries other than those it acquired in its heyday, or has it simply developed structural features that inhibit its ability to get its share of the new industries that are being born, or to profit from the locational shifts that are constantly occurring for technological and market reasons?

In our study we were driven to the conclusion that some such structural handicaps exist, which must be overcome if the region is to resume growth or even avoid retrogression.

When one compares the Pittsburgh area with other large Ameri-can metropolitan areas, certain peculiarities come to light in addi-tion to those already mentioned. Pittsburgh is more intensively specialized in a single industry than any other area of comparable size with the sole exception of Detroit. The Pittsburgh area is notably deficient, for its size, in almost all types of business services. The Pittsburgh area is characterized, to an exceptional degree, by very large industrial plants and very large firms. The labor force of the Pittsburgh area has a higher-than-average proportion of blue-collar (manual) workers compared to white-collar workers. The average educational attainment of the Pittsburgh labor force is somewhat lower than in American metropolitan areas generally. The average age and employment-seniority of Pittsburgh workers is relatively high.

We believe that all of the above facts are interrelated. Most of them can be explained directly in terms of the nature of Pittsburgh's industrial specialization to date and the slow growth history of the past several decades. I have already suggested that the relative deficiency of business services is to be explained, probably, by the prevailing large size of plants and firms as well—it is reasonable to assume that a single firm employing, say, 20,000 workers will require less in the way of outside business services, freight forwarders, and the like, than would forty separate firms employing 500 workers each. In the large firm or plant, more of such needs are met internally. The result is that the region as a whole develops a smaller complement and variety of the kinds of supporting services upon which small and new firms are particularly dependent.

We have some inkling here of a structural handicap to development of small firms and new industries. Moreover, the sources of venture capital and enterprise in an old industrial center like Pittsburgh, wedded to mammoth enterprises of national or worldwide scope, are not as easily available for starting up relatively small new types of business as they are in many other areas. Nearly all the giant corporations which have their headquarters in Pittsburgh have far-flung operations, and in some cases do little or no actual manufacturing in the Pittsburgh region at all. They no longer have any particular incentive to locate their ventures in new fields of production within the area, as they or their predecessors did in the nineteenth century when capital and enterprise were less mobile and tended to seek outlets close at hand. And holders of private fortunes built up on the basis of the industrial pioneering of previous generations are not always eager to share the risks of financing untried innovators in new fields.

Such factors help to explain why Pittsburgh, after a brilliant early record of pioneering in new industries, has in the past half century spawned so few, and missed out almost entirely in the furious burst of innovation and industrial expansion associated with electronics and space age technology. Actually, all of the leading Pittsburgh-based industrial corporations were established there more than a half-century ago—there have been no additions to their ranks since then.

The region's industrial structure has been such, then, as to generate a smaller crop of potential entrepreneurs, and also has provided less effective support and encouragement for those who might seek to start up new lines of production in the area. . . .

Those concerned with that future are placing more and more emphasis upon three main elements of a development program, all of which would sound strange to the regional industrial development proponents of even a few years ago. It is important to note that the universities of the region play a vital role in each of these three elements.

One of the three elements of the program is the drastic upgrading of the manpower supply, through improved basic education, technical training, and retraining, to make it more adaptable to present day and foreseeable requirements. A second element is a broad improvement of the physical and cultural amenities of the community to make it a more attractive place for the highly mobile and choosy types of personnel who are crucial in establishing and staffing research-based industries.

The third element, possibly the most crucial, is the creation of a regional intermediary mechanism for channeling to potential entrepreneurs three things: (1) information on the new technical possibilities being opened up by the massive research effort centered on man's exploration of space, (2) information on the specific demand for new products by Government agencies and other buyers, and (3) adequate venture capital to share the risks of innovation.

No one can say whether this effort will succeed. But I think much can be learned from the Pittsburgh region's searching analysis of its arrested growth and its bold effort to break the shackles of its past and join the twentieth century.

PART II

Who Are the Unemployed?

A PROFILE OF UNEMPLOYMENT

Joseph Zeisel

Joseph Zeisel is Economic Adviser to the U.S. Department of Labor's Office of Manpower, Automation, and Training. He has worked on a wide range of current economic problems for the National Industrial Conference Board, the Chamber of Commerce, and the Bureau of Labor Statistics and he is the author of several widely used studies, such as that on the structure of unemployment in areas of substantial labor surplus. As a recipient of the Labor Department's Distinguished Service Award, he spent a year in England studying that country's labor market policies. This excerpt from his study, Manpower and Training, *is supplemented by material from the 1964* Manpower Report *of the Labor Department.*

Some groups in the labor force are particularly hard hit by unemployment. Often they are concentrated in a geographic area where industries have declined, leaving a chronically depressed labor market. Or, in any labor market, they may be disadvantaged by reason of age, color, or lack of adequate training or education.

YOUNG PERSONS

Unemployment has always been substantially higher among young persons than among adults. In 1962, for example, the unemployment rate for labor force members fourteen to nineteen years of age was about 13 per cent; for those in their early twenties the unem-

From Manpower and Training: Trends, Outlook, Programs, Office of Manpower Automation and Training Bulletin No. 2 (United States Department of Labor, July 1963) and Manpower Report of the President, March 1964.

ployment rate was 9 per cent; but for adults twenty-five years and over it averaged somewhat over 4 per cent. Although they represent only one fifth of the labor force, young persons under twenty-five total over a third of the unemployed.

There are some obvious reasons for the relatively higher rates of unemployment for these young people. In this group are included a very large proportion of new entrants into the labor market, and they frequently have a period of unemployment associated with "shopping around" for a job. They frequently hold part-time jobs which are sporadic and occasional. Young people also tend to change their jobs more frequently than older persons as they seek the "right" job. Moreover, young people starting out on their working careers tend to be relatively vulnerable to layoffs because of lack of seniority and inexperience.

High rates of unemployment for young people have often been accepted as an inevitable by-product of a free-market economy. However, this problem has taken on increased urgency recently for several reasons.

1. Although unemployment rates have risen among all groups since 1957, the rise has been large in absolute terms among young persons. Particularly dramatic has been the sharp rise in the rate of *long-term unemployment* for young men and women in their early twenties. The rate of long-term unemployment has risen by about 50 per cent for the labor force as a whole in the past five years, but for the twenty- to twenty-four-year-olds this rate increased by more than 100 per cent.

*2. A tremendous surge of new young workers—26 million in all— will be entering the labor force in the next few years—*the result of the high birth rates of the immediate post-World War II years— putting additional pressure on the labor market.

3. There has been an acceleration in recent years of the relative decline in the number of unskilled and semiskilled jobs which usually provide first employment opportunities for new young workers.

4. There has been increased recognition that there is nothing "inevitable" about high rates of unemployment for young people. In other free-market economies, such as Great Britain, the rate of unemployment for youngsters appears to be no higher than for adults. Intensive studies of foreign labor markets have shown that adequate programs for vocational guidance, training, and placement of youth can be keys to a lower unemployment rate.

DROPOUTS

Although the rate of unemployment is high among all young people, it is far higher for youngsters who dropped out of school before graduating than for high school graduates. Dropouts differ considerably from high school graduates: a greater proportion were men, were nonwhites, and were in farm areas.

But the most dramatic of the differences is economic—27 per cent of the dropouts who left school in 1961 were unemployed in October as compared with 18 per cent of the high school graduates.

Rates of unemployment for both dropouts and graduates decline as they grow older and obtain more job experience. However, school dropouts are not able to overcome many of their disadvantages and continue to suffer from considerably more unemployment than graduates. Those who dropped out of school in 1959 had a rate of unemployment in October 1961 twice as high as that for the high school graduates of 1959. Altogether, a total of 500,000 dropouts sixteen to twenty-four years old were unemployed in October 1961, accounting for about one half of all persons in these ages who were unemployed and out of school. They accounted for about 13 per cent of all unemployed persons.

Even when they find employment, school dropouts obtain much less desirable jobs than those held by high school graduates. In October 1961, one year after attending school, some 45 per cent of dropouts were employed as laborers as compared with 19 per cent of graduates. Conversely, 41 per cent of graduates were employed in clerical occupations as compared with 11 per cent of dropouts.

OLDER WORKERS

The unemployment problem facing the older worker is often rooted in the obsolescence of his skills in a rapidly changing economy. Moreover, his problem is often complicated by lack of mobility.

The incidence of unemployment is higher for those past age fifty-five than among younger men. In 1962, for example, men fifty-five to sixty-nine years of age had an unemployment rate of 4.7 per cent, while men thirty to fifty-four years had a rate of 3.8 per cent.

Unemployment rates for men fifty-five years of age and over in the labor force have generally shown less tendency to rise during a recession. On the other hand, they have taken longer to recover. These men are better protected by seniority against layoff, but once they lose a job they face more serious difficulties in finding another. In the 1961 recovery, the unemployment rate for men fifty-five to sixty-four actually continued to rise well after the bottom of the recession had been reached.

Unemployment tends to be of longer duration as workers advance in years. Among the total unemployed, some three out of ten had been seeking work fifteen weeks or longer. This ratio was slightly less than two out of ten for teen-agers, but almost four out of ten for those forty-five to sixty-four years of age, and almost five out of ten for the sixty-five or older group. Those unemployed twenty-seven or more weeks follow a similar trend.

NONWHITE WORKERS

Throughout the postwar period the incidence of unemployment has been much heavier among nonwhite than among white workers. In 1962 nonwhites (mainly Negroes) made up 11 per cent of the civilian labor force but 22 per cent of the unemployed. More than one in ten was unemployed in 1962—an unemployment rate over twice that of white workers. Moreover, the gap in white-nonwhite unemployment rates has increased since 1957.

All youngsters have high unemployment rates. But nonwhite teen-agers have among the highest unemployment rates of any age group in the labor force. In 1962 the unemployment rate for nonwhite boys fourteen to nineteen years of age stood at 21 per cent; for girls, at 28 per cent. The comparable figure for white boys and for white girls was 12 per cent.

Despite some increase in occupational opportunities since World War II, nonwhite workers are still concentrated in relatively un-skilled work—farm and nonfarm labor, domestic service—and in semiskilled production jobs. These are also the occupational groups where unemployment rates are highest.

If the occupational distribution of whites and nonwhites in the labor force were identical, it is estimated that the difference in the over-all rate of unemployment would be cut in half. The remaining difference reflects the fact that nonwhite workers have higher unemployment rates than white workers in the same occupation group.

Unemployment spells also tend to last longer among nonwhite than among white workers. For example, on the average in 1962, about one third of all jobless nonwhite workers had been out of work fifteen weeks or longer; the comparable figure for unemployed white workers was 27 per cent. Nonwhite workers, who represented 11 per cent of the labor force and 22 per cent of the unemployed, accounted for 26 per cent of the long-term unemployed.

During postwar recessions, unemployment rose by about the same relative amount among both white and nonwhite workers from the prerecession level to the trough. During the recovery periods, however, there appears to have been a definite lag in the recovery of unemployment rates among nonwhites, both in the over-all rate of unemployment and in the extent of long-term unemployment. For nonwhite workers, the recovery not only came later; it also was less vigorous. Thus the result has been to widen the white-nonwhite disparity in unemployment in recent years. Although the nonwhite worker may not be the first to be laid off, it appears that once he loses his job he is less likely to be recalled or to find another.

UNSKILLED WORKERS

Almost every study concerned with employment and unemployment conditions points up the importance of skill, training, and education in the labor market. In the groups discussed—the young worker, the older worker, the nonwhite worker—the absence of needed occupational skills looms large in their employment difficulties. The highest unemployment rates among major nonfarm occupation groups in the postwar period have been recorded by nonfarm laborers, operatives (largely semiskilled production workers in manufacturing and machine operators in other industries) and service workers (not including professional or domestic service workers)—all relatively unskilled groups.

At the other end of the scale, unemployment rates are extremely low among professional and technical workers, and among managers, officials, and proprietors.

There is a strong relationship between education, occupation, and unemployment. With each step up the educational and occupational ladder, the rate of unemployment shows a significant drop. In March 1959 (the latest data for which figures are available) unemployment rates ranged from 10 per cent for those who did not complete their elementary school education to under 2 per cent for college graduates.

INDUSTRIES OF HIGH UNEMPLOYMENT

High rates of unemployment are, of course, not solely the result of age or color or of insufficient skill and training. Unemployment is also high among both skilled and unskilled workers in industries where employment is highly seasonal or irregular for other reasons, in industries which are particularly sensitive to the business cycle, and in industries which have shown little increase over many years in production and employment. Of course, within a given industry the skilled worker is less likely to be laid off than the less skilled.

Construction is a prime example of an industry where workers are subject to a high risk of unemployment at any stage in the business cycle. In 1963 their unemployment rate was 12 per cent, more than twice that for all workers. Construction is subject to sharp seasonal fluctuations; it is an activity characterized by short-term projects and loose attachments between employers and employees; and construction employment tends to vary sharply with the business cycle.

The unemployment rate among mine workers has been higher than the over-all average rate in each of the last fourteen years although there has been a moderate decline in the rate in recent years. This industry has been subject to a long-term reduction in jobs because of mechanization and competition from other products. Long-term unemployment has always been especially high among mine workers who lose their jobs, since mining communities tend to offer little in the way of alternative employment opportunities.

Unemployment in trade tends to run higher than for other service industries, probably because of a very high rate of turnover, and temporary attachment of many workers.

THE LOCATION OF UNEMPLOYMENT

The impact of unemployment is felt unevenly not only by different groups in the population and by occupations and industries but also by different communities. In December 1963, for example, one quarter of the one hundred and fifty major labor market areas regularly classified by the Department of Labor were listed as having relatively substantial unemployment (over 6 per cent).

Unemployment remained almost unchanged in most of the major labor market areas in 1963 with the average rate of unemployment showing no significant variation from that of 1962. But of the one hundred and fifty areas regularly classified, thirty-eight had unemployment rates above 6 per cent in December 1963 compared with forty-one in December 1962.

Many of the major areas with substantial unemployment have had persistent unemployment problems for several years. In some instances, these areas have been characterized by high unemployment levels for over a decade, in periods of over-all national prosperity as well as recessions. Chronic higher-than-average unemployment in these areas and many smaller ones throughout the nation is directly related to such factors as the shutdown of obsolete plants, the transfer of important local industries, closing of military installations, changes in consumer demand, changes in technology, or the depletion of natural resources. Local employment cutbacks arising out of these developments have been particularly severe in coal mining and in textile, steel, auto, and machinery centers.

Of the country's 3.8 million unemployed workers in December 1963, slightly less than one sixth, or about 600,000, lived in the 574 areas classified by the Department of Labor as "areas of substantial and persistent unemployment." These are areas where unemployment rates have been significantly higher than the national average for several years—in most instances at least 50 per cent higher for three of the past four years. The 574 areas of substantial and persistent unemployment, which include fifteen major labor market areas on the United States mainland, account for about a tenth of the nation's labor force and about 15 per cent of its total unemployment.

The labor market areas classified as having substantial and persistent unemployment include two of the country's principal industrial centers—Pittsburgh and Providence-Pawtucket. The Detroit area was removed from this category in mid-1963 as a result of local economic improvement stemming from increased automobile sales.

Nonfarm wage and salary employment is more heavily concentrated in manufacturing in the fifteen major areas of substantial and persistent unemployment than in the country as a whole. Manufacturing employment totaled almost 770,000 in these areas in December 1963, representing about 38 per cent of their nonfarm employment. In the nation as a whole, factory employment constituted only 30 per cent of the nonfarm total in December 1963.

This heavy dependence on manufacturing as a source of employment—with factory jobs usually centered in one or two dominant industries which have been declining or not expanding for some time (textiles, steel, aircraft, machinery, railroad equipment)—is a major contributing factor to the unemployment problems of depressed areas. In seven of the fifteen areas in December 1963, more than two fifths of the local nonagricultural jobs were in manufacturing. In only two areas was the proportion as low as 30 per cent; in both these areas one important industry—resort activities or transportation—accounts for a significant share of local employment.

UNDERUTILIZATION OF MANPOWER

Unemployment has traditionally furnished the best single measure of the effectiveness with which the economy employs its human resources. The large and persistent differentials in unemployment among various groups in the labor force provide a clear measure of their relative success or lack of it in labor market adjustment. The figures serve to quantify, often vividly, the connection between failure in this adjustment and disadvantages of educational and skill deficiencies for individual age and color groups.

However, under conditions where the economic disadvantage of individuals or groups is chronic, or where opportunities are repeatedly and inequitably denied, the statistical measure of unemployment may fall short of indicating the full extent to which manpower is not utilized in the economy. Where opportunities are chronically limited, some persons give up a fruitless search for work and rely on charity or in other ways subsist without recourse to work—and no longer are included in the statistical measure of the unemployed.

It is difficult to know to what extent this erosion of employment has been a feature of the labor market in recent years. Variations in participation in the labor force at the younger and older ages have been mainly a function of such factors as the longer schooling among the young and the alternative of voluntary retirement among older workers. The increasing withdrawal of older workers probably reflects to some degree their "squeeze-out" from the labor force during recent years of relatively high unemployment. However, statistical confirmation of the precise causes of this withdrawal from the labor force has not always been possible, and hard conclusions regarding the economic pressures leading to such withdrawal have been notably difficult to test with the information available.

In recent years, however, there have been some concrete indications that a decline in labor force participation for some groups represents a deterioration in their employment situation.

Among Negroes, labor force participation has declined significantly while their unemployment has been increasing. In the white population no significant decline in labor force rates is apparent among older men with some college education, but the rates for men with less education have edged down slightly since 1957 for those forty-five to sixty-four years of age and sharply for those sixty-five and over. The decline in the older group has been greatest among those who failed to complete a grade-school education. At any given time, low participation in the labor force, as well as high unemployment, appears to be directly connected with a limited education.

Underutilization of Negroes

The evidence of recent deterioration in the Negro employment situation compared with whites is even more graphic when the parallel trends of unemployment and declining participation in the labor force are combined. While unemployment rose between 1948 and 1963 from 39 to 78 per 1,000 nonwhite men in the central working ages of twenty-five to fifty-four, the proportion not in the labor force rose from 42 to 62 per 1,000. Among white men at the same ages, unemployment moved up from 21 to 33 per 1,000, while the proportion not in the labor force was actually reduced from 33 to 28 per 1,000. The net result of these combined effects of unemployment and departure from the labor force was an increase in those not employed from 81 per 1,000 nonwhite males (aged twenty-five to fifty-four) in 1948 to 140 per 1,000 in 1963. During the same period the equivalent figures for the white population rose from 54 to 61 per 1,000. . . .

Both the rise in unemployment and the falloff in participation between 1948 and 1963 were much sharper among older nonwhite men than among either the younger nonwhite groups or the white group of the same ages. The availability of social security benefits and private pensions cannot be the entire explanation for the decline in participation among older nonwhites. The fact that white men at the same ages showed neither the same sharp increase in unemployment (for fifty-five- to sixty-four-year-olds up from 27 to 53 per 1,000 for whites and from 33 to 105 per 1,000 for nonwhites), nor the same increase in withdrawal from the labor force (up from 104 to 122 per 1,000 for whites and 114 to 184 per 1,000 for nonwhites) prompts the conclusion that at least some of the Negroes' withdrawal from the labor force was directly connected with conditions of limited job opportunities.

The major increase in this squeeze-out from the labor force among nonwhites seems to have occurred after 1958, a year of recession from which there has been only imperfect recovery in many respects. Unemployment among nonwhites had in fact risen sharply during each of the postwar recessions, but since 1954 had failed to recover to the same extent as white unemployment rates during each subsequent business pickup. The familiar pattern of "first to be fired, last to be rehired" appears to have become "first to be fired, and possibly never rehired."

The same aggravated effects of disadvantage plague other groups of workers. The poorly educated of any race, like the Negroes, are affected in multiple ways: by higher rates of unemployment, by unemployment of longer duration, and by more frequent spells of unemployment—resulting to a disquieting extent in an ultimate discouragement that extinguishes the will of many to continue their search for work.

Education and Underutilization

The relationship between inadequate schooling and high unemployment has been shown in a number of studies. For example in 1962, workers (eighteen and over) with less than five years of school had an unemployment rate of almost 10 per cent; those who finished elementary school had an unemployment rate of about 7 per cent; high school graduates, 5 per cent; and college graduates, 1.5 per cent.

When the handicap of inadequate education is superimposed on other disadvantages, the effects are often compounded by a decline in labor force participation. An example of the degree to which a limited education deters the utilization of older workers, both through unemployment and nonparticipation in the labor force, is indicated in the statistics on educational attainment of workers in 1962. While the correlation is not perfect, it is nonetheless clear that older persons with the least education suffer both the highest unemployment and the least participation in work life; those with the most education are the most fully utilized—the most attached to the labor force and the least unemployed. White men forty-five to fifty-four years old, for example, show an employment ratio which declines from 961 per 1,000 for college graduates to 778 per 1,000 for those with less than a fifth-grade education (see Table 1.)

THE DIFFUSION OF UNEMPLOYMENT

Unemployment rates considered alone may not only fail to reveal the full extent of a deteriorating employment situation, as illustrated by the declining utilization of the Negro population and of older uneducated persons, but may also appear to show an improvement where none exists. Over the past several years, a slight pattern of diffusion in unemployment has been indicated by the moderation of unemployment rates in some industrial sectors and geographic areas where unemployment has been significantly higher than the national average, and by a relative rise in unemployment rates in a number of industries and areas of low unemployment. Between 1959 and 1963, the national unemployment rate increased only slightly (from 5.5 to 5.7 per cent) but there was some decline in mining unemployment—despite continuing contraction in the num-

Table 1

Manpower utilization of white men 45 to 54 and 55 to 64 years old,
by years of school completed, 1962
(rate per 1,000 in population)

Age and employment status	Elementary school			High school		College	
	0-4 years	5-7 years	8 years	1-3 years	4 years	1-3 years	4 years or more
45-54 YEARS							
Total not employed	221	172	135	85	78	73	39
Unemployed	84	74	64	40	24	25	10
Not in labor force	137	48	71	45	54	48	29
Employed	778	829	865	915	922	926	961
55-64 YEARS							
Total not employed	361	232	191	151	129	136	114
Unemployed	77	45	42	36	32	24	23
Not in labor force	284	187	149	115	97	112	91
Employed	639	768	809	848	871	864	886

ber of mining jobs—and in durable-goods manufacturing and transportation where there had been little or no growth in employment.
On the other hand, unemployment rates rose in trade and in the
finance, insurance, and real estate industries, both industries of
employment expansion.

Geographically, a somewhat related pattern of relative moderation
of the employment situation has been apparent in areas of high unemployment, despite stability in the over-all unemployment rate.

To some extent the improved area unemployment situation reflected increased employment opportunities in specific industries.
The rise in manufacturing employment over the past several years
has undoubtedly been a factor in reducing unemployment rates in
a number of areas, as well as for the industry as a whole. However,
in other industries, a decline in unemployment rates has been apparent since 1959, despite continued contraction in employment
(e.g., mining) or no employment increase (transportation and public
utilities).

This pattern of change in the distribution of unemployment appears to suggest some change in the nature of the unemployment problem—some moderation of the structural dislocations which have resulted in a concentration of unemployment in particular industries, labor force groups, and geographic areas. On the other hand, the lack of over-all reduction in unemployment for the economy as a whole appears to imply an offsetting rise in unemployment in other areas and sectors of the economy, reflecting a generalized inadequacy of employment opportunities.

It is not at all surprising that over a period of half a dozen years of relatively high unemployment some changes should occur in the industrial and geographic distribution of employment and unemployment. It is in the nature of a free labor market and a mobile labor force that this is so. What is important is whether these changes represent to any large extent a successful adjustment by the hard core of the unemployed to alternative employment opportunities in expanding occupations, industries, and areas. . . . Unfortunately, the data that are available on unemployment by labor force groups and by areas appear to indicate that the movement of workers out of areas and industries of high unemployment resulted in no over-all improvement in the employment situation.

The data on manpower utilization which were presented earlier in this section for Negroes and uneducated older workers suggest that part of the apparent decline in unemployment in contracting industries, occupations, and areas may represent not an improvement in the employment situation, but a squeeze-out of workers from the labor force.

Moreover, a decline in unemployment in one industry or occupation may not reflect an improvement in that sector or a reduction in its displacement tendencies, but rather a shift of unemployment to another sector. The identification of the unemployed according to their occupation and industry is frequently difficult to make in any meaningful way because the figures relate to the last job held by the worker. After a long period of unemployment, a worker laid off from a steel or aircraft plant may take what he feels is an interim job in a gas station or a supermarket. At best this represents a case of underemployment—a sharp cut in his income and less than optimum utilization of his abilities. At worst, the worker is again laid off but this time shows up as unemployed in retail trade, not in manufacturing. It is difficult to know how much of this has occurred, but the employment drop—without a corresponding rise in unemployment—in durable-goods industries which are significantly below the 1957 job level—e.g., in transportation equipment, down by 250,000; machinery, down by 100,000; and steel down by 100,000—suggests that the transfer of unemployed to other industrial sectors, rather than improvement in employment, has been the significant factor in reducing unemployment in these specific sectors during the past several years.

The adjustments that have been made in the last several years apparently have not resulted in any significant improvement in the employment position of those groups in the labor force hardest hit by unemployment—the uneducated, the unskilled, youth, and nonwhites. As noted earlier, the relative employment position of each of these groups has at best remained unchanged and in some cases deteriorated. Of course, the shifts out of industries and areas of high unemployment that have occurred undoubtedly avoided a further deterioration in employment for these groups.

The employment picture for geographic areas appears to reflect the same patterns. A study of the employment history of twelve major labor market areas in which the unemployment rate has been persistently at least two points higher than the national average in four of the last seven years shows a decline of 3.8 per cent in unemployment in these areas, despite a sharp increase (23 per cent) for the 113 major labor market areas as a group. However, this relative improvement in their unemployment situation during this period, as compared with the 113 areas under study, was associated with a decline in the labor force rather than improved employment opportunities. Between 1957 and 1963, the aggregate work force in the high unemployment areas *declined* by about 220,000, or 6 per cent, as compared to an *increase* of nearly 8 per cent in all of the areas under study; employment in these areas declined by over 6 per cent between 1957 and 1963, as compared with an increase of 7 per cent for all of the areas (see Table 2).

The evidence of population changes for most of these areas between 1950 and 1960 suggests that outmigration, and not significantly improved employment opportunities, was responsible for moderating the rise in unemployment within the areas and, moreover, may have contributed to the relative worsening of other areas. A study of a sample of areas of high and persistent unemploy-

Table 2

Employment, unemployment, and total work force in 113 major labor market areas and in 12 areas of relatively substantial unemployment, 1957 and 1963
(numbers in thousands)

Employment status	113 major labor market areas[1]		12 areas of relatively substantial unemployment[2]		Per cent change, 1957-63	
	1957	1963[3]	1957	1963[3]	113 areas	12 areas
Total work force	31,021	33,400	3,532	3,314	7.7	−6.2
Total unemployed	1,369	1,687	235	226	23.2	−3.8
Total employed	29,652	31,713	3,297	3,088	7.0	−6.3

[1] Areas classified by the U.S. Department of Labor on the basis of adequacy of labor supply for which comparable data are available for the period 1957-63.

[2] Areas with unemployment rates two percentage points above the national average in at least four of the past seven years.

[3] Preliminary (eleven-month) average.

ment during the decade of the 1950's supports these conclusions and indicates that the outmigration occurred almost entirely among young adults (aged twenty-five to forty-four), the most mobile and adjustable members of the labor force. Older workers and younger members of the population continue to be concentrated unduly in these areas.

These data would seem to indicate that no significant change has occurred during the past several years in the nature of the unemployment problem facing the nation. Individuals may no longer be identified to the same extent as previously with declining industries, such as mining or some manufacturing industries, and some may have migrated from depressed areas; but the labor market disabilities which too frequently caused their unemployment and hindered their re-employment in the past apparently continue to do so. On the other hand, those workers with a good education or possessing contemporary skills, and who are not handicapped by discrimination because of age or color, have had comparatively little difficulty in adjusting to the structural changes which occur.

WORK HISTORY, ATTITUDES, AND INCOME OF THE UNEMPLOYED

Robert L. Stein

Robert Stein is Chief of the Division of Employment and Labor Force analysis in the U.S. Department of Labor's Bureau of Labor Statistics. In addition to his basic studies on unemployment and job mobility, on the part-time labor force, and on the extent and nature of frictional unemployment, he has been centrally responsible for preparing the monthly report on employment and unemployment conditions that provides a common source for the writers, politicians, economists, and other controversialists tilting about economic policy.

In April 1962 . . .[the] Bureau of Labor Statistics surveyed an estimated 9.6 million workers eighteen years old or older who experienced at least five full weeks of unemployment in 1961 * (counting all spells of unemployment). . . .

Of the 9.6 million unemployed, nearly 70 per cent were men— the vast majority in the prime working years of twenty to sixty-four (Table 1). Family heads accounted for three fifths of the unem-

From *Work History, Attitudes and Income of the Unemployed,* United States Bureau of Labor Statistics Special Labor Force Report No. 37 (1963).
* The survey included persons unemployed five weeks or more in 1961 who were eighteen years or older in April 1962, able to work, not in school, and who had some prior work experience. Collection and processing of the data were conducted by the Bureau of the Census under contract with the Bureau of Labor Statistics. About 3000 personal interviews with sample respondents were completed. In each case, the person who actually experienced the unemployment was interviewed. For a more detailed account of this survey, see *Monthly Report on the Labor Force* (March 1963), xiv-xxi; (May 1963), 16-24; (August 1963), 15-27.

Table 1

Labor force attachment during 1957-61 of persons unemployed 5 weeks or more in 1961,[1] by sex and duration of employment in 1951
(Per cent distribution)

Labor force attachment	Total	Men	Women	Duration of unemployment in 1961	
				5-26 weeks	27 weeks or more
In labor force all year[2] 1961	77.9	84.0	64.2	74.4	89.8
In labor force every year, 1957-60	60.4	68.9	41.2	58.3	67.5
All year, every year	46.9	55.3	28.1	46.0	50.2
All year, 3 years	8.9	9.8	6.9	8.1	11.6
All year, 2 years or less	4.6	3.8	6.2	4.2	5.7
Out of labor force 1 year, 1957-60	5.8	5.0	7.6	5.6	6.7
Out of labor force 2 years or more, 1957-60	11.7	10.1	15.3	10.5	15.7
In labor force part year, 1961	22.1	16.0	35.8	25.6	10.2
In labor force every year, 1957-60	12.0	9.9	16.6	13.6	6.5
Out of labor force 1 year, 1957-60	2.2	1.6	3.6	2.5	1.3
Out of labor force 2 years or more, 1957-60	7.9	4.4	15.7	9.5	2.4
Per cent of persons	*100.0*	*100.0*	*100.0*	*100.0*	*100.0*
Number of persons (thousands)	*9,617*	*6,606*	*3,011*	*7,345*	*2,272*

[1] Includes persons 18 years old or older in April 1962 who were able to work, not in school, and who had some prior work experience.
[2] "All year" is defined as 50-52 weeks.

NOTE: Because of rounding, sums of individual items may not equal 100.

ployed, and nonwhite workers for one fifth. A fourth of the group suffered more than six months of unemployment in 1961. Only a third of the unemployed, compared with over half the civilian labor force, were high school graduates.*

* See "Educational Attainment of Workers, March 1963," *Monthly Labor Review* (May 1963), 504-15.

WORK HISTORY

Labor Force Attachment

In April 1962, 67 per cent of the 9.6 million workers who were unemployed five weeks or more in 1961 were back at work,* while another 26 per cent were looking for work. Only 7 per cent had left the labor force. . . . The proportion of women who were no longer working or seeking work was larger than that of men—15 per cent compared with 3 per cent.

. . . Even among men forty-five years old and over . . . , only 6 per cent were not in the labor force at the time of the survey.

Of the . . . workers who had left the labor force, half . . . intended to look for work again—most of them within a month of the . . . interview . . . ; 36 per cent did not plan to rejoin the labor force, mainly because of ill health or household responsibilities; and 13 per cent were undecided as to whether they would seek employment. . . . Those not planning to look for a job because they thought no work was available amounted to only 3 per cent of those not in the labor force in April 1962. . . .**

To determine whether the unemployed were regular or occasional members of the labor force, the survey . . . obtain[ed] a five-year work history of these workers. The data indicate that this group's attachment to the labor force . . . [proved to be] relatively strong. Nearly 80 per cent were either employed or seeking employment all year (defined as 50-52 weeks) during 1961 (Table 1). Over the five-year period, nearly half the group were in the labor force all year every year.† These findings must be considered only rough

* The fact that a high proportion of the unemployed were back at work should be interpreted with caution because this status relates only to a single week. Preliminary data for a subsample of 1000 persons interviewed in both 1962 and 1963 about their unemployment experience in 1961 and 1962 revealed that some 52 per cent had at least a month or more of unemployment in both years.

** Persons who reported "no work available" or "could not find work" were so classified, regardless of other reasons reported.

† A study of persons claiming benefits under the Temporary Extended Unemployment Compensation Program (TEUC), conducted by the Bureau of Employment Security of the U.S. Department of Labor in 1961 and 1962, found that 75 per cent had been in the labor force continuously for the past three years. The difference results from several factors: (1) since the period covered by the Bureau of Labor Statistics study was longer, a lower propor-

approximations. . . . (Many persons were unable to recall accurately the details of their employment and unemployment over this period. . . . Furthermore, some of the unemployed in 1961 were too young to have worked during part of the period. . . .

About 55 per cent of the men were in the labor force all year each year, whereas only 28 per cent of the women reported such consistent participation. . . . [Two thirds of the] men who were forty-five years old and over in April 1962 (2.2 million of the 9.6 million covered) . . . were in the labor force all year every year. Only 8 per cent were out altogether for one full year or more.

Unemployment Record

Unemployment was . . . [no] new experience for most of the persons covered by the . . . survey. Only about a third reported no unemployment during 1957-60.

Table 2

Per cent of workers who experienced specified unemployment during 1957-60

	Total	Men	Women
No unemployment	31.0	27.1	39.9
Unemployment in 1 year only	21.0	19.9	23.4
Unemployment in 2 years	15.8	16.8	13.8
Unemployment in 3 years	10.5	11.5	8.0
Unemployment in each year	21.8	24.7	15.0
Total	*100.0*	*100.0*	*100.0*
Number of workers (thousands)	*9,617*	*6,606*	*3,011*

NOTE: Because of rounding, sums of individual items may not equal 100.

Those with long spells of unemployment in 1961 had . . . somewhat more unemployment in previous years; in addition, they were

tion with continuous labor force activity would be expected; (2) a much larger proportion of the Bureau of Labor Statistics sample of all unemployed were under twenty-five years of age—23 per cent compared with 12 per cent of the TEUC recipients—and had therefore entered the labor force only recently; (3) certain unemployed workers not covered by the unemployment insurance system and not eligible for TEUC (agricultural and domestic workers) are much more likely to move into and out of the labor force; and (4) unemployed workers with insufficient wage credits in covered employment to qualify for benefits would typically be intermittent members of the labor force.

twice as likely to be out of work in April 1962 as were the others.
Nearly half the persons with six months of unemployment in 1961
were also unemployed in April 1962.

About 3.2 million of the 9.6 million unemployed in 1961 had no
job in April 1962; 80 per cent of these people were looking for work,
and only 20 per cent—mostly women—had stopped looking.

Of the 3.2 million workers without a job, 73 per cent indicated
conditions such as slack work, work not available, or job completed
as the principal reasons why they were no longer at their last
jobs. . . .

Occupational and Industrial Experience

In terms of movement between occupations and industries, the
. . . workers included in this study were relatively mobile. . . .
About 40 per cent were in a different major occupation group (and
40 per cent in a different industry group) at the end of the five-year
period. About 20 per cent of the workers reported an occupation
other than their last as their best job—as defined by the respondent.
The figures for industry groups were fairly similar.

Despite this extensive occupational and industrial turnover, however, the distributions of first, best, and last jobs held by these
workers were remarkably similar. . . . Apparently a substantial part
of the shifting was offsetting rather than in one consistent direction.
Between best and last jobs, a slight downgrading tendency could be
observed. . . .

. . . Only 22 per cent of the 9.6 million workers reported a white-
collar occupation even for their best job, whereas over 40 per cent
of all employed workers in each year from 1957 to 1962 were in
these occupations. Moreover, between first and last jobs, there was
no rise in the proportion in white-collar occupations among the 9.6
million, whereas for employed workers it has been steadily rising.

RESPONSES TO UNEMPLOYMENT

Methods Used to Find Work

The work-seeking activities of unemployed persons are sometimes
taken as an index of the intensity and seriousness with which they

are job-hunting. All persons in this survey reported use of at least one standard method, and 87 per cent used two or more. Over 75 per cent of all the unemployed checked with a state employment office and with local employers—the methods most frequently used. Resorted to somewhat less frequently were the placing or answering of ads and the writing of letters of application. Checking with friends and with a union or a private employment agency were not often used.

Expectation of Recall

Of the 3.2 million persons not employed at the time of the survey, 1 million stated they anticipated recall to their last job. Half . . . expected to return within a month, and an additional third expected to return within one to three months. Eighty-three per cent said it depended on an incerase in business activity; half were seasonal workers awaiting a seasonal pickup. Duration of unemployment apparently had only a minor effect on expectations of recall. The proportion of those with over six months of unemployment who anticipated recall (28 per cent) was nearly as high as for those with shorter periods (34 per cent).

Type of Job Sought

A very high proportion of the unemployed, including over four fifths of those expecting to be recalled, looked for another job—a full-time job in almost all instances. Almost half of those who had not looked for another job were women, most of whom had withdrawn from the labor force.

By and large, the unemployed were seeking jobs with relatively low skill requirements. About two thirds reported they were looking for jobs in the semiskilled operative, service, or unskilled laborer categories (including those who stated they wanted "general work in a factory" or "any kind of work"). Only 12 per cent sought jobs as skilled craftsmen, while 20 per cent wanted white-collar jobs (mostly in the clerical field). These latter proportions were not far out of line with the proportions whose last jobs were in these occupations, as indicated in the following tabulation:

Table 3

(Per cent distribution)

	Job sought by persons without a job in April 1962 who looked for work	Last job of all persons without a job in April 1962
Professional, technical, and kindred workers	2.1	1.4
Managers, officials, and proprietors	.9	2.8
Clerical and kindred workers	13.0	10.9
Sales workers	3.7	4.7
Private household workers	4.3	4.4
Service workers, except private household	10.5	13.7
Craftsmen, foremen, and kindred workers	12.3	13.7
Operatives and kindred workers	18.9	29.5
Laborers, except mine[1]	11.5	18.9
General work in factory	2.6	....
Any kind of work	20.1	....
Total	*100.0*	*100.0*
Number of workers (thousands)	*2,869*	*3,175*

[1] Includes a small proportion of farm workers.

NOTE: Because of rounding, sums of individual items may not equal 100.

Wages desired by persons not at work were moderate. The median was slightly over $60 per week, about the same as . . . they earned on their last job. Persons not expecting recall wanted a weekly wage of less than $60; on the average those expecting recall sought jobs paying $70, about the same [average] as recorded for the 6.4 million persons employed at the time the survey was taken.

Potential Mobility

Among the group who anticipated recall, . . . 80 per cent indicated they would definitely accept another job in their home area (Table 4). In marked contrast, if the job were in another part of the country, only 26 per cent would definitely take it. . . . Persons who did not expect to return to their last job had similar attitudes to-

Table 4

*Willingness of persons unemployed 5 weeks or more in 1961,[1] who were
unemployed or on layoff in April 1962 to accept a job similar to lost job
in same and another area, by sex and duration of unemployment in 1961*
(Per cent distribution)

Job area and response	Total	Men 18 to 44 years old	Men 45 years old and over	Women	Duration of unemployment in 1961 5 to 26 weeks	Duration of unemployment in 1961 27 weeks or more
Persons expecting recall (thousands)	*1,014*	*419*	*263*	*330*	*689*	*325*
Job in same area:						
Total	*100.0*	*100.0*	*100.0*	*100.0*	*100.0*	*100.0*
Yes, definitely	80.4	87.3	78.9	72.5	78.7	83.8
Yes, it depends	11.1	9.9	11.1	12.8	11.7	9.9
No	8.5	2.8	10.0	14.7	9.6	6.3
Job in another area: Total	*100.0*	*100.0*	*100.0*	*100.0*	*100.0*	*100.0*
Yes, definitely	26.0	35.4	28.6	12.2	22.4	33.1
Yes, it depends	21.7	29.9	26.4	7.8	21.6	22.0
No	52.3	34.7	45.1	80.0	56.0	44.9
Persons not expecting recall (thousands)	*2,161*	*640*	*598*	*926*	*1,334*	*827*
Job in another area: Total	*100.0*	*100.0*	*100.0*	*100.0*	*100.0*	*100.0*
Yes, definitely	26.7	37.4	36.8	13.3	24.2	30.4
Yes, it depends	17.7	17.6	27.9	11.5	18.6	16.4
No	55.6	45.0	35.3	75.2	57.2	53.2

[1] Includes persons 18 years old or older in April 1962 who were able to work, not in school, and who had some prior work experience.

NOTE: Because of rounding, sums of items may not equal totals.

ward accepting employment away from home. . . . The proportion definitely willing to move was highest among men under forty-five years of age who were not expecting recall (37 per cent). Most persons who would not accept a new job elsewhere gave family and home ties in their present community as the reason. Persons whose unemployment was of long duration indicated a slightly greater willingness to move to another area than persons whose unemployment was of shorter duration.

INCOME AND LIVING STANDARDS

Government statistics on unemployment measure the extent of unutilized labor immediately available in the economy; they have never been intended as a measure of financial need or hardship. . . . The extent to which unemployment affects . . . workers and their families . . . [depends] on such factors as the position of the unemployed person in the family, the duration of his unemployment, and his eligibility for unemployment insurance. . . .

Personal Income

The average income from all sources for . . . persons unemployed a month or longer in 1961 was $2,300. This was nearly 40 per cent below the $3,700 average for all other persons with income who had some work experience during the year.* Moreover, the . . . median income of the long-term unemployed was only about $1,400, or a little over half that of those unemployed from one to six months.

Persons employed all year primarily at full-time jobs averaged $5,000; but only one out of every eight unemployed persons had an income of that size or greater. However, only part of this difference can be ascribed directly to . . . unemployment . . . : even when the jobless were employed, their average weekly earnings were considerably lower than those of year-round full-time workers. On their current or last job, the . . . unemployed earned about $70 a week; the comparable weekly wage or salary for year-round full-time workers during 1961 was roughly $95. This gap arises from the lower educational levels of the unemployed, their greater concentration in the less skilled and lower paying occupations, and their more frequent part-time work weeks. . . .

---

* Averages in this discussion are medians based on distributions of persons with income. Comparative income data were derived from "Income of Families and Persons in the United States: 1961," *Current Population Reports,* Series P-60, No. 39 (Washington, D.C.: U.S. Bureau of the Census).

Despite the effects of unemployment, about 80 per cent of the income received by unemployed persons in 1961 came from their own wages and salaries. Another . . . 12 per cent was derived from unemployment insurance. The remaining 8 per cent was obtained . . . principally from welfare and pension programs. . . .

Wage and Salary Income

During 1961, wage and salary income of the 9.6 million unemployed averaged about $1,900, compared with nearly $5,000 for year-round full-time workers. Nevertheless, even for persons with unemployment, wages and salaries were the most important source of income; 95 per cent received at least some wage income during 1961, whereas only 69 per cent received income from other sources.* The average wage income was three and one-half times larger than the average income from other sources.

. . . Nearly 90 per cent of the long-term unemployed had at least some wage income during the year. . . . In the aggregate, a little over half the total income of the long-term unemployed came from wages and salaries.

Unemployment Insurance

Unemployment insurance was an important, although only partial, offset to the loss of wage income during 1961. Slightly more than half . . . of the unemployed . . . received unemployment insurance benefit payments.** Of those who did not receive these payments, most had not applied for them, presumably because they were not eligible. The median weekly benefit was about $36. The median period for those receiving compensation was about fourteen weeks, half of the maximum duration allowable in most states (not counting temporary extensions, such as those provided in 1958 and 1961). Most of the unemployed apparently found jobs before the

---

* The proportion of the unemployed who received other types of income was considerably larger than for the population as a whole (49 per cent), but smaller than the proportion receiving wage income.
** These statistics . . . are subject to sampling variability and errors of reporting. For this reason, and because of differences in coverage, the data are not entirely consistent with administrative records from the unemployment insurance system.

expiration of their right to regular and extended benefits; however, one fifth did exhaust their benefits during 1961.

Among those jobless twenty-seven weeks or more in 1961, unemployment insurance benefits were of great significance, averaging almost 10 per cent more than their 1961 earnings from wages and salaries. In fact, one out of nine of the long-term jobless had no wage or salary income in 1961. . . .

Income from Other Sources

. . . The proportion of unemployed persons receiving such income ranged from the 8 per cent who obtained supplementary unemployment benefits to the 1.5 per cent who received private pensions. About 4.5 per cent of the 9.6 million with unemployment received income from social security which averaged close to $700 annually—the largest amount from any single source other than wages.* In fact, income from all sources other than wages and salaries averaged only a little over $500 during 1961. Moreover, . . . these . . . amounts . . . were calculated on the base of those who received $1 or more of such income. Thirty per cent had no such income at all.

Even for the long-term unemployed, wages and unemployment insurance were by far the most important sources of income. For this group, however, social security benefits and public assistance were relatively more significant than for those unemployed for shorter periods of time.

Dependency Status

Although concern for the well-being of the family unit is raised whenever a member becomes unemployed, the situation is most serious if the unemployed person has others dependent on him. The majority . . . of the jobless were family heads, financially responsible for other persons.** Another 25 per cent were unrelated indi-

* These payments were not necessarily received during a period of unemployment; the income data relate to amounts received at any time during the calendar year.

** A study of persons claiming benefits under the TEUC program, conducted by the Bureau of Employment Security in 1961 and 1962, found that 62 per cent were primary earners. Of these, 14 per cent lived alone. Primary earners are persons who, when queried, stated they usually provide the main support for their families.

viduals or family members who took care of their own living expenses. The remainder were mostly wives of family heads . . . ; a very small proportion . . . were family members who did not provide for their own living expenses (Table 5). About three fifths of

Table 5

Family status of persons unemployed 5 weeks or more in 1961,[1]
by sex and duration of unemployment in 1961, April 1962
(Per cent distribution)

| | | Men | | | Duration of unemployment in 1961 | |
| | | 18-44 years old | 45 years old and over | | 5-26 | 27 weeks |
Family status	Total			Women	weeks	or more
Heads, spouse present[2]	48.8	66.3	80.5	. . . .	51.0	41.8
Heads, other marital status[2]	6.3	1.9	3.7	14.8	5.9	7.8
Wives	16.8	. . . .	. . . .	53.8	17.3	15.2
Other relatives	19.5	26.5	4.6	20.3	18.4	23.1
Provided for own living expenses	16.7	22.9	4.3	16.8	15.8	19.7
Did not provide for own living expenses	2.8	3.6	.4	3.5	2.6	3.4
Unrelated individuals	8.5	5.3	11.2	11.1	7.4	12.1
Per cent of persons	100.0	100.0	100.0	100.0	100.0	100.0
Number of persons (thousands)	9,617	4,404	2,202	3,011	7,345	2,272

[1] Includes persons 18 years old or older in April 1962 who were able to work, not in school, and who had some prior work experience.
[2] Includes heads of subfamilies.

NOTE: Because of rounding, sums of individual items may not equal 100.

the . . . married women who were unemployed had children under eighteen. . . .

The effect of unemployment of the family head on the family situation was mitigated somewhat in those families in which other members had jobs. In one third of the families which included a wife or other relative 18 years old or over, someone else in the family was employed at the time the family head suffered his first stretch of unemployment in 1961; in most instances his wife was the other worker. [In only 12 per cent of the families] did the unemployment of the family head induce other family members [(usually the wife)] to enter the labor force.

Family Income and Living Standards

In 1961, the average family income of the 8.8 million unemployed persons in families* was $4,400. . . . The 8.8 million . . . included 5.3 million family heads—almost 90 per cent of them married men, wife present. Most of the following discussion deals with families in which the unemployed person was the head.

The average income of these families was $4,100, compared with . . . $6,900 for families in which the head was a year-round full-time worker. . . . [These] differences cannot be taken as an indication of the effect of the head's unemployment alone. As noted earlier, the weekly earnings of all persons with unemployment (when employed during 1961) were $25 lower than those of year-round workers; if a similar gap is assumed for family heads, it would imply an annual difference of $1,300, apart from the effects of unemployment. Assuming further that the weekly earnings of unemployed family heads ($75 to $80 a week) were somewhat higher than for the unemployed as a whole, their average loss of potential earnings through unemployment could be estimated at about $1,100 to $1,300,** since their average duration of unemployment was about fifteen to sixteen weeks. Roughly two fifths of this loss was offset by unemployment compensation for the 3.4 million heads who received these benefits.

* The unit of measurement in this analysis is the unemployed person by the characteristics of his family. In a small number of cases, more than one person in the same family was unemployed a month or longer during 1961; thus, the total number of families involved is slightly smaller than the number of family members.

** Precise data on the average weekly wage and salary earnings during 1961 of heads with and without unemployment are not available. On their current or last job, all persons with unemployment averaged $70 in weekly earnings. Average duration of unemployment for family heads jobless more than five weeks during 1961 was estimated from "Work Experience of the Population in 1961," *Bureau of Labor Statistics Special Labor Force Report No. 35,* Table C-1.

Despite his loss of earnings through unemployment, the family head's wage income was a major component of his family's income. During 1961, the head's wage income ($2,700) accounted for nearly three fifths of aggregate . . . income for these . . . families. . . . Nonwage income of the head, principally from unemployment insurance benefits, and the earnings of other family members . . . [made up the remaining] two fifths of . . . aggregate income.

Since the earning ability of the head tends to exceed that of other family members, his unemployment strikes a much greater blow at the family's financial solvency than does the joblessness of other members. Among the 3.5 million families in which the unemployed person was the wife or other relative, family income averaged $800 more than for the 5.3 million families in which the head was unemployed. . . .

. . . In about one fourth of the 3.5 million families in which the unemployed person was the wife or other relative, these family members provided more than half the family's wage or salary income in spite of their unemployment. Of course, their loss of income while unemployed had a serious effect upon the financial structure of their families.

Number of Dependents

Sharing the total income of families with an unemployed head were an estimated 19 million persons . . . : 5.3 million family heads, 4.7 million wives, 8.5 million children under eighteen years old, and 600,000 dependent relatives and other persons. Families with an unemployed head not only had incomes about . . . two fifths lower than for families whose heads had steady full-time employment, but they were also faced with the need to distribute their lower income among relatively more consumers. For example, among the families affected by the head's unemployment, some 26 per cent had three children or more under eighteen . . . ; whereas among other families, 22 per cent had three children or more. . . . [And although 64] per cent of the families hit by unemployment had young children, [only 59] per cent of the other families were in this position.

Among the families with an unemployed head, the total income available rose as family size increased. . . . This reflects the contribution of additional earners plus the fact that the head's earning power reaches a peak in his late thirties and early forties. However, in families with more than five persons the increases in income were slight and per capita income dropped sharply.

How Living Expenses Were Met

. . . Almost half the families . . . [reduced] their savings, averaging $400 (Table 6). Nearly one quarter of the families borrowed

Table 6

Methods used by family to meet living expenses during unemployment, by family position of unemployed person[1] and duration of unemployment, 1961
(Per cent distribution)

Method	Total	Heads	Wives and other relatives	Unrelated individuals	5 to 26 weeks	27 weeks or more
			Family position of unemployed person		Duration of unemployment in 1962	
Used savings	46.9	51.0	36.9	52.5	49.1	39.9
Median amount	$396	$441	$261	$356	$378	$443
Borrowed money	22.6	26.9	16.8	12.7	23.7	18.8
Median amount	$308	$347	$288	$195	$315	$281
Moved to cheaper housing	9.5	11.2	6.6	8.5	8.8	12.0
Sold property	4.3	4.3	4.7	3.4	4.3	4.5
Received help from friends or relatives outside the household	19.1	19.8	15.3	27.5	18.0	22.5
Received cash assistance from public or private welfare agencies	7.4	7.7	7.2	6.8	5.6	13.2
Received other public assistance	11.4	13.9	8.0	5.5	9.1	18.7

[1] Includes persons 18 years old or older in April 1962 who were able to work, not in school, and who had some prior work experience.

NOTE: Sum of per cents adds to more than 100 because many families resorted to more than one method.

money, with half of the borrowers obtaining $300 or more. Other
means . . . included cash assistance and surplus food from . . .
welfare agencies and moving to cheaper housing. Each of these
methods was resorted to . . . where the jobless person was unemployed more than twenty-six weeks.

Table 7

*Income in 1961 of families with members unemployed 5 weeks or more,
by type of income, median amount, and aggregate distribution*

Family member and type of income	Families receiving specified type of income		Median income	Distribution of aggregate family income
	Number (thousands)	Per cent		
All families with head unemployed	*5,301*	*100.0*	$4,148	*100.0*
Head's total income	5,296	99.9	3,200	71.8
Wage and salary income	4,976	93.9	2,686	58.2
Nonwage income	4,121	77.7	596	13.5
Other members' total income	3,328	62.8	1,470	28.2
Wage and salary income	3,081	58.1	1,546	25.9
Nonwage income	666	12.6	635	2.3
All families with wife or other member unemployed	*3,500*	*100.0*	$4,988	*100.0*
Unemployed person's total income	3,367	96.2	1,370	28.0
Wage and salary income	3,284	93.8	1,139	23.2
Nonwage income	1,817	51.9	411	4.7
Other members' total income	3,383	96.7	4,266	72.0
Wage and salary income	3,359	96.0	4,374	65.7
Nonwage income	1,006	28.7	1,010	6.4

NOTE: Because of rounding, sums of individual items may not equal 100.

Table 8

*Personal and family income in 1961 of persons unemployed 5 weeks or more,
by family position and duration of unemployment*

Family position and duration of unemployment	Total (thousands)	Median income		Personal as a per cent of family	Per cent who received or whose families received—	
		Personal	Family		Under $3,000	$7,000 and over
All persons	9,617	$2,300	$4,153	55.4	33.8	17.8
Persons in families	8,801	2,347	4,413	53.2	29.6	19.4
Heads	5,301	3,209	4,148	77.4	31.1	15.6
Others	3,500	1,370	4,988	27.5	27.2	25.4
Unrelated individuals	816	1,825	....	....	76.3	1.8
UNEMPLOYED 5 TO 26 WEEKS						
All persons	7,345	2,607	4,418	59.0	30.2	19.8
Persons in families	6,804	2,649	4,619	57.4	26.7	21.3
Heads	4,176	3,562	4,421	80.6	27.6	17.4
Others	2,629	1,607	5,086	31.6	25.4	27.7
Unrelated individuals	541	2,160	....	....	71.1	2.7
UNEMPLOYED 27 WEEKS OR MORE						
All persons	2,272	1,443	3,279	44.0	45.9	11.0
Persons in families	1,997	1,450	3,636	39.9	39.9	12.7
Heads	1,126	1,984	3,253	61.0	44.8	8.6
Others	871	833	4,638	18.0	33.2	18.1
Unrelated individuals	276	1,357	....	....	87.0	....

NOTE: Because of rounding, sums of individual items may not equal totals.

PART III
Recent Programs, Here and Abroad

Since 1961 the federal government has begun three major programs to reduce unemployment. One, the tax cut, was intended to reduce joblessness stemming from inadequate demand. Two others were intended to cope with the problems of retraining workers and reconverting areas to better meet the needs of the future. These last two programs are reviewed in the present section.

TRAINING PROGRAMS FOR THE UNEMPLOYED

Sar Levitan

Sar Levitan has studied and dealt with manpower problems in various capacities—as a staff member of the Joint Economic Committee, as a college teacher, and now in his position with the respected Upjohn Institute for Employment Research. For this discussion he draws upon his experience in helping to draft the Area Redevelopment Program.

. . . Since 1961 the federal government has inaugurated two new programs aimed largely at training and retraining unemployed workers. The underlying rationale for these programs is the assumption that despite the high level of unemployment which has prevailed during recent years there are many unfilled vacancies because the unemployed are not properly prepared to fill the job openings. Justification for the new training programs is clearly expressed in the preamble to the Manpower Development and Training Act:

From *Federal Manpower Policies and Programs to Combat Unemployment* (Kalamazoo, Michigan: Upjohn Institute for Employment Research, 1964). Used by permission of the author and the Upjohn Institute.

The Congress finds that . . . even in periods of high unemployment, many employment opportunities remain unfilled because of the shortage of qualified personnel; . . . it is in the national interest that current and prospective manpower shortages be identified and that persons who can be qualified for these positions through education and training be sought out and trained. . . .

ARA PROVISIONS

The training provisions of the Area Redevelopment Act, enacted in 1961, are part of a package of tools provided by Congress to aid areas of high chronic unemployment. Under the provisions of the Area Redevelopment Act, unemployed persons selected for training are eligible to receive up to sixteen weeks' subsistence payments, equal to the average unemployment compensation benefits paid in the state where the workers receive training.

MDTA PROVISIONS

The Manpower Development and Training Act, enacted in 1962, is much broader in scope. It provides for a maximum training period of fifty-two weeks. Trainees are also eligible to receive extra daily subsistence or transportation allowance if they are selected to attend courses outside the commuting area of their regular place of residence. Training under the Act was largely limited to unemployed heads of families who had had three years' experience in the labor market. Youths between the ages of nineteen and twenty-two were eligible to receive a maximum of $20 a week training allowance. Younger youths were eligible to receive training but not subsistence benefits. Training allowances paid to youths were limited to 5 per cent of total expended training allowances. However, experience has shown that demand for training by youths below the age of twenty-two exceeded congressional expectations, and in December 1963 Congress amended the Manpower Development and Training Act to make youths between the ages of seventeen and nineteen eligible for training allowances. As a result, youths below the age of twenty-two may now constitute one fourth of all persons receiving training allowances.

Other 1963 amendments included the following provisions:

1. The federal government will pick up the complete tab under the MDTA program until July 1, 1965, and two thirds of total costs during the following year. The original law required state matching of federal funds beginning with July 1, 1964. The authorized federal expenditure for training during fiscal 1965 was raised to $407 million from the original $161 million; the federal share will be $271 million for fiscal 1966. Whether Congress will actually increase the appropriations is not known at the present time.
2. As a special incentive to induce unemployed workers who are collecting unemployment compensation to undertake and complete retraining courses, the amendments permit raising the weekly allowance paid to trainees to a maximum of $10 above the average state unemployment compensation payment. Experience has shown that many unemployed workers have not taken advantage of the training provisions as long as they have been eligible to receive unemployment compensation and that others have discontinued training before completing the course.
3. To encourage underemployed workers to pursue training and to encourage trainees to complete their courses of training, provision was made to permit trainees to work part-time (up to twenty hours per week) without any loss of training allowances.
4. Training in basic education may be included as part of the vocational course for those who lack a rudimentary education, and the training period for them may be extended to a maximum of seventy-two weeks. Experience under the ARA and MDTA has shown that many workers would benefit from such a training program.
5. Workers' eligibility qualifications for training were reduced to two years' prior work experience; and when the head of a family is unemployed, another member of that family may receive a training allowance. . . .

INSTITUTIONAL TRAINING PROJECTS

The bulk of training under MDTA and ARA has been carried out in publicly financed vocational education institutions. However, the 1963 MDTA amendments permit greater leeway in utilizing private training facilities. Since little time was available for planning once Congress appropriated funds for ARA and MDTA training, most of the projects are based on course curricula designed for traditional vocational education programs; and normally the same facilities and instructors are used. Additional federal funds have made it possible, however, to modernize and expand training equipment. . . .

Training projects have been approved in some 450 different occupations. The most popular occupations for which training courses have been approved to the 128,000 selectees under ARA and MDTA programs as of December 1, 1963, included stenography, typing, and general office work; machine operating; nursing (practical licensed nurses and nurses' aides); automobile mechanics and repairing; and welding. The five occupational groups accounted for half of the total training. . . .

DEMONSTRATION PROJECTS

Many hard-core unemployed are not likely to benefit from established training techniques. These may include youths who are school dropouts and who have had unusual difficulty in finding or holding employment, older workers with a low educational attainment, and the physically or mentally handicapped. . . . To help such disadvantaged individuals, . . . the Department of Labor has . . . been forced to bypass the vocational education facilities and to provide for the rehabilitation of the disadvantaged groups through community social work centers. For example, a Chicago project is designed to train a thousand presumably unemployable youths (many illiterate) "to reach the necessary educational level for employment, to develop the attitudes required for employment, to acquire some job skill experience, and finally to be placed in employment." Almost half of the registrants were on relief and 40 per cent had achieved less than a sixth-grade reading ability. . . .

Altogether, by December 1963 . . . [the Department of Labor] had approved twenty-eight demonstration projects involving some 30,000 individuals. Thus far only a small proportion of the trainees have been selected for training. Most of the projects involve youths, but several are also aimed to help adults. . . .

A summary of key figures for the MDTA program is provided

by the following table, which is based on data from *Report of the Secretary of Labor on Manpower Research and Training* (1964).

Manpower Development and Training Act Projects, 1963

Institutional projects	
Persons trained in 1963	27,000
Persons to be trained in fiscal 1964	60,000-70,000
Average weekly maintenance allowance	$36
Average weeks of training (per trainee)	23
Average cost of training and maintenance (per trainee)	$1,355
Percentage of 1963 trainees who, at time enrolled—	
received unemployment insurance	25%
received public assistance	8%
were unemployed	89%
Total projects approved in year	
costs of training (in millions)	$61.7
costs of maintenance allowances (in millions)	$65.8
On-the-job training projects	
Persons trained in 1963	736
Persons to be trained on projects undertaken in 1963	6,733
Average cost per trainee on projects approved in 1964	$550
Total costs (in millions) on projects approved in 1964	$4.2
Demonstration and experimental projects	
Persons trained in 1963	32,270
Costs (in millions)	$5.0

RETRAINING THE UNEMPLOYED:
A PRELIMINARY SURVEY

Gerald G. Somers

Gerald Somers has specialized in the problems of the labor market as Director of the Institute of Industrial Relations at the University of West Virginia, and now as Professor of Economics at the University of Wisconsin. His extensive analyses and field studies of labor mobility in depressed areas have provided much of our basic knowledge on these problems.

The conclusions reached by a number of critics of retraining are disheartening. They are disheartening not because retraining lacks potential for long-run good, but because the programs to date appear to have had such limited short-run impact on the hard core of unemployment. The disillusionment is greater because the initial expectations were so high. In the various Congressional hearings on unemployment policies, retraining proposals met with an almost "unanimous chorus of praise." After all, training is education, and who can be opposed to education? Training is the vehicle for occupational mobility, and in a dynamic economy of structural change who can be opposed to mobility?

But the expectations and current experience must both be seen in perspective. Retraining has three major objectives: (1) short-run increase in employment; (2) long-run economic growth; (3) improvement in the welfare and general well-being of the trainees and society. Regardless of any short-run deficiencies, there can be little doubt that retraining the unemployed, like the educational process

From a statement made before the Senate Subcommittee on Employment and Manpower and reprinted from the Committee's *Hearings*, Part 2, (June 4-7, 1963).

as a whole, is a worth-while enterprise from the standpoints of the long-run economic growth of the American economy and the general well-being of its citizens. Indeed, some authorities are now saying that the investment in human resources, through education and training, has accounted for a greater part of our economic growth than the investment in capital equipment. Even if immediate employment does not result, the acquisition of new skills and knowledge by the unemployed is likely to make some future contribution to their own advancement and that of the economy.

Retraining allowances will usually take the place of unemployment compensation or relief payments for unemployed workers. Even if there were small additions to the costs for society, in what better way can the unemployed spend their moments of enforced idleness than in the acquisition of new skills? Our research provides ample evidence that retraining can give a new sense of pride, confidence, and social status to unemployed workers; and these represent substantial social gains regardless of immediate labor market consequences.

Therefore, one may well favor a greatly expanded program for retraining of the unemployed even if it could be demonstrated that no immediate jobs were created thereby. But most of those who have supported recent retraining measures have been more concerned with the current problems of unemployment than with long-run growth and well-being. And herein lies the disillusionment. The short-run concern can be seen in the Manpower Development and Training Act provisions which restrict retraining to those who have a "reasonable expectation of employ"; in the incorporation of retraining provisions in the Area Redevelopment Act's attack on depressed areas; in the inclusion of retraining to meet the dislocation which may result from the Trade Expansion Act; in the retraining provisions espoused in the youth conservation bill; and in the many state and local efforts to reduce relief rolls through retraining.

IMMEDIATE EMPLOYMENT EFFECTS OF RETRAINING

It is clear from national statistics as well as our own surveys that government-subsidized retraining has achieved only minor reductions in unemployment to date. This is primarily because of the limited period of experience with retraining, the small scale of the

enterprise, and the state of the economy. In small part, the poo
showing stems from deficiencies noted in a number of criticisms o
the current programs; and our own research, although still in proc
ess, supports many of these findings. Some deficiencies are minor
They are recognized by the training authorities and can be correctec
with the passage of time. Our responses from trainees, employers
unions, and government officials indicate that some of the curren
Area Redevelopment Act and Manpower Development and Trainin\$
Act courses are too short for the occupational objectives they seek tc
achieve; equipment is often inadequate in quantity and quality, anc
frequently it is available to unemployed trainees for only a fev
hours in the evening; instructors may be out of touch with the lates
techniques; training allowances are often inadequate; retrainec
workers are not provided the tools which they are expected to brinj
to the job; local advisory committees have not always functionec
effectively; and the complicated relations between the Office of Man
power, Automation, and Training, the Bureau of Employment Security, and [the Department of] Health, Education, and Welfare—
both in Washington and at the local level—have sometimes served
to delay the inception of programs and impair their effective functioning.

However, these are growing pains; many of these problems are
now being solved and they can be expected to diminish further as
greater experience is gained. The relatively meager accomplishments
of the retraining programs to date are basically attributable to the
fact that they have just begun, but the real concern for their future
success stems from more fundamental causes.

The crucial issues are (1) whether the retraining programs are
currently enrolling the hard core of the unemployed, and (2)
whether sufficient job vacancies now exist to justify a substantial
lowering of selection standards.

The answer to the first question clearly depends on one's definition
of *hard-core unemployment*. The national data indicate that the
Area Redevelopment Act and Manpower Development and Training
Act trainees include more long-term unemployed but fewer older
and less-educated workers than are found among the unemployed
as a whole in the areas from which they are drawn. This has led
some to recommend that selection standards be lowered so as to include more hard-to-place workers. From the standpoints of long-run

economic growth and general well-being this would be justified; but such a lowering of standards would probably lead to a lower placement ratio in the present status of the economy.

Even under the present selection standards the placement ratio of Area Redevelopment Act trainees is 65 per cent and of Manpower Development and Training Act trainees, 70 per cent, according to national data sources.

. . . Our West Virginia surveys provide some preliminary findings concerning the employment experience of those who completed Area Redevelopment Act and West Virginia retraining courses relative to those who were found unacceptable for referral to training, as well as to those who did not report for training following their acceptance and those who dropped out of the training course prior to its completion. The tables also indicate the significance of the passage of time as an influence on employment experience following retraining. . . . Whereas only 37 per cent of the workers who had not been referred to training were employed one month following completion of the training course, 47 per cent of those who completed training had found employment by this time. Workers who did not report for training after they had been accepted were only slightly more likely to be employed one month after the training course ended than those who were found to be unacceptable. On the other hand, workers who dropped out of the training course prior to their completion had an even higher placement ratio (53 per cent) than workers who completed the training course. This is attributable to the fact that many of the dropouts withdrew in order to take a job.

As time elapses following completion of the training course, all of the sampled groups improve their employment status, but it is notable that the workers who completed the training course make a more substantial improvement with the passage of time than those who dropped out prior to completion. . . . Approximately nine months after the initial interview surveys . . . workers not referred to training continued to have employment rates well below those enjoyed by workers who had completed training in each of the three areas.

. . . A notable finding is that a relatively large proportion of the trainees withdrew from the labor force in the months following their training. Of those who completed their training course, 9 per cent were no longer in the labor force three months following the course. . . . Those whose applications for training had been rejected had especially high rates of nonlabor-force status. . . . Nineteen per cent of the workers who had completed their training course in the Huntington area were no longer in the labor force in April 1963, at least nine months after the course completion.

These high rates of withdrawal from the labor force may result from a paucity of employment opportunities, but they may also reflect a lack of commitment to the labor market among many of the workers selected for retraining. The tendency for trainees to withdraw from employment—and, often, from the labor force—is especially noticeable in such training occupations as nurses' aides and waitresses. These are often cited as shortage occupations, but the chronic shortage may very well reflect low wages, undesirable working conditions, and high turnover. The work histories of many of the women attracted to these training courses reveal only a marginal attachment to the labor force. It must be assumed that in some cases the training allowance serves as a principal inducement for retraining in low-level service occupations.

In surveys we have conducted in Harrison and Monongalia Counties, West Virginia, one fourth of the nurses' aides and waitresses who had completed their training courses in those occupations were no longer in the labor force at the time of the initial interview. On the other hand, very few of the male trainees (4.4 per cent) had withdrawn from the labor force following completion of their course.

ATTITUDE OF NONTRAINEES

The differential employment experience of trainees and nontrainees can be illuminated by reference to the preliminary data on attitudes of nontrainees, drawn from the West Virginia surveys. . . . Those who applied for retraining but were found unacceptable felt overwhelmingly that they could have done the work in the training occupation to which they aspired. Only 4 per cent indicated that they were not qualified. Almost all of these so-called rejects took the general aptitude tests administered by the Employment Service, and three fourths felt that the tests were fair in spite of their disqualification.

A surprisingly large proportion of workers do not enroll in a training course after having been accepted on the basis of their test results and interviews; 36 per cent of these did not report for training because they found employment prior to the beginning of the course. . . . Because of limitations in training facilities or prospective employment opportunities, 27 per cent could not be accommodated in the training course.

For dropouts, too, the temptation of an immediate job is a major factor in their decision to withdraw from the retraining program. . . . Dropouts were especially numerous under the West Virginia area vocational program because trainees do not receive a weekly allowance during training under this program.

AGE AS A SELECTIVE FACTOR

Nonaccepted applicants for retraining are considerably older than those who are referred to the courses by the Employment Service. . . . In one area of West Virginia almost half of the "rejects" were over forty-five years of age in contrast with only 14.6 per cent of accepted applicants. The higher age of the "rejects" contributes to their failure to pass the aptitude tests and also serves as an independent factor causing their rejection by Employment Service counselors. Thus the youth of trainees in government programs, relative to the average of the unemployed, can be explained only in part by the lack of motivation of older workers. Even those who are sufficiently well motivated to apply for admission to a retraining course are less likely than younger workers to have their applications accepted.

RETRAINING AND RELOCATION

Relocation of retrained workers will frequently be necessary if the retraining investment is to bear fruit in job placement. This is especially true of retraining in depressed areas. It is not always recognized that the acquisition of new skills through a retraining program is in itself a powerful inducement to move out of an area of limited employment opportunities. In the study of McDowell County, West Virginia, a depressed coal mining area—it was found that almost one third of the trainees under a State program for the unemployed had moved out of the county by the time of the interview survey. We managed to track down over one hundred of the West Virginia outmigrants through mail questionnaires and personal interviews. In a preliminary tabulation, over 40 per cent indicated that their decision to move had been influenced by their training. However, only half of these were employed, as compared with over 60 per cent of the total outmigrant group and roughly the same percentage who find employment under all Area Redevelopment Act retraining programs.

One lesson to be learned here is that the major role of relocation allowances could be not to induce more outmigration but, rather, a more rational outmigration. By making the allowance contingent upon a move to known job opportunities, much fruitless geographic movement could be avoided. A second lesson is directly related to the planning of training programs in depressed areas. Less than 3 per cent of the outmigrants were over fifty years of age. Training courses for unskilled older workers are most effective in low-service occupations, geared to local opportunities. Younger workers in depressed areas can benefit from training in welding or some of the expanding occupations which presuppose their migration to areas in which industrial growth is taking place.

ON-THE-JOB AND TRAINING
FOR SPECIFIC EMPLOYERS

The immediate employment effects resulting from government-subsidized retraining could be enhanced by subsidized on-the-job training. . . . A number of the Area Redevelopment Act retraining programs have been so closely geared to the needs of a single employer that they provide a useful experience by which to judge some of the advantages—as well as some of the pitfalls—of on-the-job training for the unemployed.

The immediate job-placement record of retraining will obviously be greater if the unemployed are assured of employment in a designated firm even before they are trained. The trainee benefits in morale and the employer is provided with employees trained to the specifications of his particular job. The subsidy to the employer embodied in government-financed retraining can be a more direct and more attractive inducement to his expansion of employment opportunities when he gains greater control of the retraining procedures and content. Our surveys indicate that many employers, especially in such service occupations as auto repair and nurses' aides would prefer this type of arrangement. Almost 40 per cent of the employers preferred government subsidies for on-the-job training over the use of vocational school facilities, as now generally practiced under the Area Redevelopment Act and the Manpower Development and Training Act. . . .

But caution must be observed to insure that much of the training is extended to unemployed workers and not only to the upgrading of existing employees. Our analysis indicates that many employers might prefer to use the government-subsidized retraining provisions in ways which offer little benefit for the hard-core unemployed. An analysis of several Area Redevelopment Act training programs in West Virginia and elsewhere, where courses have been designed to fill the needs of a specific employer, indicates that the job-placement ratio is considerably higher than average, but that the selected trainees are younger and better educated than other Area Redevelopment Act trainees. In some of these firms, all of the employed trainees are under forty-five and have . . . a high school education.

Care must also be taken to see that employees are assured some continuity of employment after their government-subsidized on-the-job training. Workers trained for a specific job in a specific plant will be placed in a vulnerable position if they are again set adrift among the unemployed. There have been some unfortunate experiences along this line under Area Redevelopment Act programs geared to a specific employer.

HUMAN INVESTMENT IN LONG-RUN ECONOMIC GROWTH

Although the preceding discussion has been couched primarily in terms of the short-run employment function of government-subsidized retraining, it is desirable to conclude with the long-run values of retraining with which this statement began. If retraining is to make its maximum contribution to the attainment of full employment and long-run economic growth, it will be necessary to broaden selection standards to include more older, less-educated, and minority-status unemployed. But the Employment Service must not then be judged by the traditional standards of an immediate job-placement ratio.

Our surveys indicate that the trainees, themselves, take the long-run view. Most undertake retraining not simply to obtain any job, but to obtain a better job than they have known in the past, one which can be more secure and more productive.

NEW OPPORTUNITIES FOR DEPRESSED AREAS

John D. Pomfret

The following excerpts are from a comprehensive report by John D. Pomfret, of The New York Times, *on the Area Redevelopment Act, which he terms "a modest yet promising effort to shore up the sagging economies" of our depressed areas.*

. . . Hunger and despair stalk these valleys. In some counties, a third of the people are "on commodities"—the government's surplus food dole. There is no hope that the mines ever will re-employ the thousands of idle men, nor is there other work for them to do.

The situation in eastern Kentucky is perhaps the worst in the country. Here bands of desperate pickets, disowned by the United Mine Workers of America, roam the hills, harrassing and sometimes dynamiting the small nonunion mines where their hunger-driven fellow miners work for pay far below the union scale.

The tragedy involves more than the visible victims—the unemployed and their families. This enforced idleness exacts a fearful price from their communities in the form of relief costs, ungarnered taxes on income that is never earned, and depleted public facilities. It runs up the employers' unemployment compensation bills and deprives them of business. It works a hardship on the whole nation through wasted manpower that could be put to use building needed schools and hospitals, rehabilitating its cities or restoring its land, producing goods or providing services.

. . . An irony of the situation is that advocates of special measures to aid the depressed areas were able to prevail on Congress

From *New Opportunities For Depressed Areas* (New York: Public Affairs Committee, Inc., 1963). Used by permission of the author and the Public Affairs Committee, Inc. Copyright © 1963 by the Public Affairs Committee, Inc.

to pay attention to their problems only when the nation as a whole was suffering from so high a rate of unemployment that it was difficult to attack the plight of the depressed areas in an effective way. The federal tax, credit, and expenditure measures necessary to restore full employment in the nation at large are, if anything, even more essential for the sake of the depressed areas.

. . . What does the Area Redevelopment Act provide and what is its philosophy? Essentially, it is a package of tools designed to help depressed communities help themselves attract and foster industial and commercial concerns. It relies largely on local initiative. Its most important emphasis is on encouraging depressed areas to assess and mobilize their own resources for economic growth.

. . . The package of tools which the Act authorized include:

1. Loans—not to exceed $100 million in rural sections—for industrial and commercial purposes, including buying land, erecting buildings, and purchasing equipment. The money can be borrowed for up to twenty-five years. The current rate is 4 per cent. The money must not be available from other sources on reasonable terms. A loan may not exceed 65 per cent of the total cost of a project, excluding working capital. ARA money cannot be used for working capital. At least 10 per cent of the project's financing must come from the state or community or local redevelopment agency and at least 5 per cent must be from nongovernmental sources. These shares cannot be repaid until ARA has been paid back. No loans may be made to assist pirating of industrial facilities from one community to another, and "dozens" of applications have been rejected on this ground, according to the ARA.

2. Public facility loans—also not to exceed $100 million in outstanding obligations—for development of public facilities to improve the opportunities for getting or expanding industry or commerce. These loans can be made for up to forty years. The present rate is 3⅝ per cent. Again, funds must not be available from other sources at reasonable rates.

3. Grants—of $75 million—for similar public facilities to fulfill a pressing need where there is little probability that the project can be undertaken without the grant. Grants usually are used to make up the difference between what can be secured from other sources, including ARA loans, and the cost of the project.

4. Annual authorization of $4,500,000 for technical assistance—for

studies to evaluate the needs of communities and develop the potentialities for their economic growth.

5. A program run by the Labor Department and the Department of Health, Education, and Welfare to retrain jobless workers in depressed areas. Expenditures of $4,500,000 a year are authorized to pay for the training and $10 million to pay for allowances for trainees for up to sixteen weeks in an amount equal to the average weekly unemployment benefit in their state.

But the central feature of the Act is its provision that, to be eligible for its other benefits, an area must first submit and win approval of an over-all program for economic development. Projects, to gain approval, must be consistent with this plan.

The plan is the heart of the ARA program. It is the tangible embodiment of the ARA's philosophy: That the main impetus for redevelopment must come from the depressed area itself.

. . . What have been the results of the ARA program so far? In some cases, remarkable.

One example is that of Johnson County, Tennessee. It was in the agricultural doldrums because its small hill farms could not compete with big, mechanized rivals. Unemployment was widespread and so was underemployment. Younger people were leaving. Between 1950 and 1960, the population dropped from 12,278 to 10,765, and most of those who left were from fifteen to thirty-nine years old.

A group of community leaders decided they had to try to reverse this pattern of disintegration. They formed the Johnson County Industrial Commission and floated a $400,000 county bond issue to create a thirty-acre industrial park and build a plant.

The Area Redevelopment Act was passed and the county was duly designated a redevelopment area. The local group, with the help of the University of Tennessee Cooperative Extension Service and the United States Department of Agriculture, drew up an OEDP (i.e. development plan). Sixteen separate committees composed of about two hundred local people looked at all aspects of the county's economic problem. Agriculture, natural resources, manufacturing, recreation, education, and conservation were surveyed.

ARA loaned the county $60,000 and granted it another $46,300 to provide water and sewage facilities to finish the industrial park. A garment manufacturer moved in, providing employment for 204 workers and an annual payroll of $500,000. Assistance is now being sought to get other employers started. The county is making plans for a new high school and working to develop its attraction as a tourist center.

"The ARA program served as a catalyst in bringing about these developments," the community group reported recently. "It provided the incentive for the people to come together as a coordinated group and look at the present situation, discuss the problems, and make plans for action."

The unemployment statistics indicate that Johnson County still has some distance to travel before it can claim prosperity, but it is on its way.

. . . Not only would a better general employment picture vastly improve ARA's chances for success, it would spike the guns of one of the most effective arguments of opponents of the program. They have been saying that with unused plant capacity commonplace around the country, plants established with ARA aid simply take business away from existing plants and spread unemployment, not reduce it.

Even though ARA's funds are supposed to be only seed money, with the main investment to be left to private enterprise, many observers feel that the agency has been given too little seed.

The magnitude of the task it faces is enormous. A crude estimate, making optimistic assumptions about the dimensions of the current economic upswing, indicates it would take 800,000 more jobs in chronic labor-surplus areas to bring their unemployment level down to a tolerable 4 per cent. This could mean an investment of something like more than $6 billion.

. . . One major problem ARA has encountered is the inability of many communities whose resources have been exhausted in the long battle with poverty to raise the 10 per cent in state or local funds required by the Act as their share of industrial or commercial projects. Only six states help.

. . . What is really troublesome is what to do about a depressed area that is lacking local leadership and initiative when the ARA program depends almost entirely on these for results.

A county planning board in North Carolina summed up its predicament recently in a poignant letter to ARA.

"Our success has been rather limited in enlisting able and willing people to work on further development of our OEDP," the board said. "The few people we have with competence in the field of economic planning are all busy making a living. Federal agencies are trying to be helpful. The wide dispersal among so many agencies of the possible sources of help is, from our standpoint, an unfortunate, time-consuming handicap.

. . .Even so, Mr. Batt [ARA's administrator] is optimistic.

"There is life in almost all of these areas," he says. "They are determined to survive. There is entrepreneurship there, too, although not enough in all of them, to be sure. The applications we have gotten indicate that a real need was there, and what these people needed was something to work with. I was sure these resources would be made use of if they were made available. Of course, there is a different calendar for solving the problem in almost every community. . . . This problem didn't happen quickly, and it won't be solved quickly. You don't diversify in a hurry."

RECENT SWEDISH LABOR MARKET POLICIES

Carl G. Uhr

Carl G. Uhr's work on Swedish economic policy reflects his extended study of the country of his birth. He has been Director of Research for the study Commission on California's unemployment insurance, and has written about the work of Knut Wicksell, one of the century's great economists—and personalities. Uhr is Professor of Economics at the University of California at Riverside.

EMPLOYMENT IMPACT OF THE 1958 RECESSION IN SWEDEN AND IN THE UNITED STATES

In that downturn the Swedish Labor Market Board proved capable, without having to ask for emergency appropriations from Parliament, of marshaling powerful industrial as well as governmental employment-creating measures. . . . These measures gave work to approximately 2 per cent of the Swedish labor force in the trough of that recession, the winter 1958-59. As a result unemployment, which was comfortably low at about 2 per cent in 1956-57, was kept from rising beyond 4 per cent during 1958-59, and then receded rapidly in the recovery of 1960 to its 1956 levels. After that, unemployment was reduced further and labor scarcities developed in the moderate boom which Sweden enjoyed in 1961 and 1962.

Yet, without the timely application of certain policies by the Labor Market Board, unemployment in Sweden may readily have reached 7 per cent, or more, as it did in the United States in 1958. Without the countermeasures used the Swedish recovery might, like ours, have been both slower and incomplete. . . .

From *Hearings of the United States Senate Subcommittee on Labor and Public Welfare,* Part 3 (June 18-28, 1963).

SWEDISH COUNTERCYCLICAL EMPLOYMENT POLICY AND ACTION

Besides its very important day-to-day functions, . . . the Swedish Labor Market Board has been given powers to enable it to meet a business downturn. . . . The board has the responsibility of . . . advising the national government, the employer associations, and the trade unions as to the timing and scope of action to be taken under the following measures:

1. *Activation of standby government appropriations for public works.* These appropriations, included in the annual budgets, are to be used only when the labor market situation, as indicated by the board, calls for such action. They are then spent on a variety of preplanned public works projects largely for the benefit of local governments, which do the preplanning. These projects are by no means of the make-work type. They involve expansion and improvement of public facilities which would be undertaken in any case but at another time. To the extent that they are postponable, these projects would be scheduled for later action in a tight labor market, but they are now moved ahead in a business downturn to take up the slack in a period of declining labor demand. The projects on which standby appropriations were spent in 1958-59 were for school building, road construction, drainage, water works, and forest conservation activities.

2. *Accelerating government procurement orders to private industry for military as well as nonmilitary purposes.* The aim in this case was to take up some of the slack in the Swedish engineering industries due to a temporary decline in exports.

3. *Releasing private "investment reserve funds" for use for broadly specified purposes by industry.* These funds represent profits set aside by private firms under certain tax inducements during earlier prosperous years. Initially from 1949, and on a greater scale from 1955 on, 40 per cent of net profits could be set aside tax-free, for the time being, by private firms as an "investment reserve," and of this allocation 40 per cent had to be deposited by them in special accounts in the Central Bank. These reserves and accounts were to accumulate and be held off the market in an inflationary period and until their release for industrial use was announced by the labor market board.

The incentive to private industry in accumulating such reserves is both the temporary tax relief this device affords and the provision that when the funds are released in a downturn, 10 per cent of the amounts so released can be deducted from taxable profits. If the accumulating funds are not released for use over a succession of years owing to continuous high prosperity and inflationary pressure in the economy, provisions exist for returning them to industry in gradual steps. However, in that event the funds are desterilized without any accompanying partial tax concession.

By 1958, these accumulated reserves corresponded to about 5 per cent of aggregate annual private investment spending. In 1958 and 1959 about 80 per cent of the accumulations were released for use. At that time they generated a welcome and significantly greater rise in private investment activity, respectively of 8 and 6 per cent in 1958 and 1959. After 1959 no more releases were made; instead, new and more rapid fund accumulations were invited by additional liberalization of the tax-writeoff inducement offered.

4. Acceleration of private residential and industrial building starts and provision of certain basic credits for their finance. Through its twenty-five provincial offices the labor market board controls the issuance of building permits. This control has the purpose of limiting construction work in boom times to the maximum number of units which can be built with the available construction labor supply. Control of construction activity was set up after the war to cope with Sweden's housing shortage. The controls serve to prevent the construction industry from pirating labor on a large scale from other equally vital industries, as it threatened to do in the early postwar years. In a downturn more construction labor than usual becomes available; hence building activity can then be expanded. In the 1958 recession building starts were increased by the board's actions by about 15 per cent, and corresponding amounts of low-interest mortgages covering a portion of the construction cost were provided from government loan funds.

COSTS AND IMPACT OF COUNTERCYCLICAL POLICY

The costs of these programs were relatively modest. The accelerated procurement and activation of standby appropriations for preplanned public works increased the Government's current budget outlays in 1958 and 1959 by about 8 or 9 per cent.

The release of private "investment reserve funds" amounted to about 4 per cent of private investment spending and generated a rise of 8 per cent and 6 per cent in private investment activity in 1958 and 1959.

The acceleration of housing construction added further to the positive effect of the foregoing measures. . . . The combined effect was to generate about 2 per cent more civilian employment than would otherwise have been available, and, the recession notwithstanding, the Swedish gross real national product increased rather than decreased by approximately 5 per cent between 1958 and 1959.

SWEDISH POLICIES FOR COPING WITH STRUCTURAL UNEMPLOYMENT

The problems of structural as distinct from cyclical changes in the Swedish labor market are dealt with by what I referred to earlier as the labor market board's day-to-day functions. The board:

1. Administers the country's network of public employment offices,

2. Supervises the activity of the few private employment services which remain in operation,

3. Controls and dispenses state subsidies for the payment of unemployment compensation, which is administered by the private or trade union unemployment insurance societies, and

4. Pursues industrial location research and consultation activity on a local and a regional basis for the benefit of private industry as well as for local governments.

1. Labor market placement and information activity

In performing these functions the labor market board becomes a central source of vital and current information. It receives detailed daily data on the state of the labor market because almost all vacancies are listed with its employment offices, where also all claimants to unemployment compensation are registered. In addition, Swedish employers are obliged to forewarn the board of impending layoffs by notice two months in advance of the event. About 80 per cent

of all employment-placements in Sweden are affected by the direct
or indirect intermediation of the board's employment service network.

The value of the labor market information and communication
that the board provides locally, regionally, and on a nationwide
basis can hardly be overestimated. By comparison we make much
less intensive use of the potential services and resources of the U.S.
Employment Service.

2. *Measures to stimulate geographic mobility of labor*

Structural and localized unemployment is dealt with by the measures available to the board to stimulate geographic mobility in the
labor force and to reduce barriers to occupational mobility by providing extensive programs of vocational training and retraining.

Workers living in labor-surplus areas are induced by a system of
allowances to move to available jobs, known to the employment
service, in labor shortage areas. Unemployed persons who need and
want to move over great distances to job opportunities in other
locations may apply for and receive travel expenses to seek new
work in these areas. If they locate jobs, they may immediately receive a "starting allowance." This is in substance a grant which
becomes repayable in part only if they do not hold the new job for
at least ninety days. The "starting allowance" equals the amount of
unemployment benefits they might have collected over a period of
three to four weeks of compensated unemployment.

If housing for their families is not available in their new work
location, they may receive "family allowances" for the separate
maintenance of wife and children for up to nine months in their
former location. These allowances pay the rent for the family up to
a maximum figure, plus a cash allowance for the maintenance of
wife and children. The cash payments are approximately equal to
two thirds of what the moved-away breadwinner would have obtained in unemployment compensation. For the first three months of
separate maintenance these allowances are paid in full. For the
second three months they are paid at 67 per cent of their full
amount, and for the last three months at 33 per cent. When the
family moves to the new location, its removal expense is also reim-
bursed up to a certain maximum amount.

Reports by the labor market board indicate that in the course of a year about 0.3 to 0.4 per cent of the civilian labor force make use of one or more of these geographic mobility allowances. As the Swedish Finance Minister put it recently: "It is cheaper to move manpower to jobs than to move industries into labor-surplus areas. For about 1 million in allowances of various types we can usually move almost 1,000 men and their dependents."

Finally, for removal to remote areas where housing is entirely inadequate, the labor market board supplies temporary, easily assembled, prefabricated housing for incoming workers. After that, the board, with its liaison with the construction industry and local governments, arranges for construction of permanent housing.

3. Measures for increasing occupational mobility and training

An expanding program of vocational training and retraining with unemployment compensation maintenance for trainees is now available to Sweden's unemployed. At present as many as 1 per cent of the labor force can be accommodated in this program in the course of a year, and facilities are being developed to expand these services further.

Participation in beginning as well as advanced training and retraining courses covering a wide variety of blue- and white-collar occupations is on a voluntary basis. However, retraining is strongly recommended for older workers among the long-term unemployed (persons who have been unemployed at least two months). Training is also urged for unemployed youths, especially for recent, unskilled entrants to the labor force, and particularly for the school dropouts among them.

Vocational guidance and training of a more general type and not supported by unemployment compensation is now also available to Sweden's school population as a part of the regular curriculum in the compulsory nine-year general elementary schools. It is also a part of the curriculum in the "continuation" schools provided for the majority of young persons who, having finished elementary school, do not gain entry into the country's liberal arts and technical secondary schools (gymnasia).

For handicapped and partially employable workers, the labor market board has available vocational rehabilitation programs and certain types of "sheltered employment." In the latter, handicapped workers obtain jobs at market wage rates but usually under special limiting conditions, as to time, supervision, and so on, suitable to their state of health and training. Finally, for persons hard to place in open market jobs and persons who are unwilling to undergo or are unsuitable for retraining, there are some varieties of "archivist and clerical employment" available at minimum wage scales at the agencies and offices of local governments. It seems that these types of work are mainly offered to older women workers, particularly older single women, widows, and the like, with some past office work experience.

4. Industrial location research and counseling

The labor market board is also engaged in local and regional industrial location research, analysis, and counseling for the benefit of private employers and local governments alike. This is a part of the effort to cope with localized rather than general problems of unemployment and manpower utilization. The aim of the location research is to provide the data and to prepare the community facilities needed to induce private firms to locate in labor surplus areas where a suitable labor supply is available. This function of the board is no doubt a positive factor among others in Sweden's manpower utilization policy, but it is difficult to form a reliable measure or picture of its scope and efficacy.

CONCLUDING COMMENT

We in the United States have not as yet developed as comprehensive and coordinated a set of labor market policies and institutions as have evolved in Sweden.

At the same time, it is clear that already we have available (not least by recent legislation) most of the "parts" for an effective labor market policy "machine" or apparatus. Admittedly, some of these "parts" are designed on too small a scale to be assembled into a apparatus of the size and scope required to function effectively in our highly diversified economy. This is clearly the case, for instance, with the provisions for vocational training and retraining as well as removal allowances under the present Manpower Development Act.

It is also true that we have nothing comparable to the Swedish "private investment reserve funds" subject to certain special tax writeoffs. I am not sure whether we should contemplate the use of this particular device for stimulating private investment in counter-cyclical fashion. But whether this device or some other may be developed, there is no doubt that we need to develop some method which introduces countercyclical behavior in several of the main tributaries to the private investment stream. This is needed chiefly for the reason that our "built-in stabilizers" are not powerful enough to reverse a cyclical swing, although they are capable of damping its amplitude and probably of shortening its duration.

Nonetheless, even if we enlarge the scope of various employment-stabilizing, unemployment-counteracting, and growth-stimulating programs already in existence, for effective functioning it is essential not only to enlarge them, but even more to coordinate them. To achieve the desired coordination does not require the creation of some superpowerful economic policy council or committee. But it may require the creation of some coordinating agency of Cabinet status, with powers and responsibilities like those of the Swedish Labor Market Board, and with close liaison with other appropriate departments as well as with the major economic policy committees of the Congress.

The recent experience in Sweden shows how substantial are the real benefits that derive from the functioning of such a coordinating agency for economic policy. It also shows how such an agency can be developed without impairing, but rather strengthening, the democratic institutions we want at all costs to preserve. Finally, it also demonstrates how this can be achieved without requiring any significant expansion of the scope and authority of government over the private-enterprise economy.

SELECTED EUROPEAN PROGRAMS FOR EXPANDING EMPLOYMENT

Joint Economic Committee
Congress of the United States

The Joint Economic Committee is the nom de plume *of the world's largest class in economics, in which astute and overworked Congressmen and Senators take turns being pupils and instructors to most of the nation's economists. This particular summary was prepared by Sar Levitan, John Lehman and James Knowles, then members of the able staff of the Committee.*

LOANS

Belgium:

Government guaranteed low-interest loans from quasipublic and government-approved private lending agencies available for—
  (1) Construction or remodelling of buildings or the purchase of equipment.
  (2) Financing intangible investments, such as research.
  (3) Facilitating conversion to new types of production.
  (4) Reconstitution of working capital depleted by comparable investment at an earlier date.
Government subsidy to lending institutions equivalent to difference between prevailing commercial interest rate and rate charged the borrower, up to maximum of 4 per cent. During periods of recession interest rate charged may be reduced to minimum of 1 per cent. Reduced rates generally applicable for five years, exceptionally for eight years.

From the United States Congress, Joint Economic Committee's *Selected European Programs for Expanding Employment in Areas of Relatively High Unemployment* (1960).

Denmark:

Direct government loans and private-loan guarantees available for construction of plant and installation of machinery; present fund of DKr50 million ($7 million) available.

Loans and loan guarantees available up to 90 per cent of the cost of permanent installations and machinery; up to 45 per cent of the purchase price of machinery used in rented industrial sites.

Loans for factory buildings repayable over fifteen years; for machinery, over ten years.

Government loans also available for the construction of industrial centers for lease to small enterprises. . . .

Federal Republic of Germany:

Five types of direct government loans are available:

(1) For the establishment of new plants at 3½ per cent for fifteen years provided that at least one factory job is established per $2,300.

(2) For expansion and modernization of established plants at 5 per cent for fifteen years.

(3) General measures for promotion of industry including public utilities and roads (municipal and county) and extension of vocational training facilities at 2 per cent for twenty years. These loans are limited to nonprofit corporations.

(4) For tourism—4 per cent for fifteen years.

(5) For improving agricultural productivity—at 2 per cent for twenty years.

France:

Government loans available both for land, plant and equipment, and for working capital requirements. Interest rates are variable, but are generally close to the prevailing open-market rate. Repayment period also variable but generally comparable to amortization schedules of investment loans from commercial sources.

Government loan guarantees may be available for part or all of a loan contracted from a private source.

Great Britain:

Government loans available to industries. Terms highly variable, including no fixed limit on amount of loans.

Loans generally from 50 per cent to 100 per cent of capital required. May be used for purchase of land, construction of plant, or purchase of equipment. Repayment period averages ten to twenty years. Principal, interest, or both may be deferred for several years. Loans also available for improvement of basic services in any development area. Loans made to either public or private organizations.

Italy:

Federal government loans available up to about 70 per cent of total capital needed for new plants locating in the development area or expanding facilities.

For small (up to 100 employees) and medium-size (100-500 employees), rate of interest charged to entrepreneur is 3 per cent with the government paying the difference between actual rate and normal rate of interest. Maximum duration of loan fifteen years. Maximum loans 3000 million lira ($1 equals approximately 625 liras).

Northern Ireland:

Government may undertake special plant construction according to specifications of new enterprise. Repayment terms negotiated.

Sweden:

Government loan funds primarily designed for small and medium-size enterprises (up to fifty employees). Do not exceed SKr50,000 ($10,000). Government loan funds reach private industrial enterprises through provincial industrial associations composed of all businesses in a particular area.

Government loans designed to assist small industries in general. Only [a] minority of loans made to industries locating in labor surplus areas.

Government funds lent to provincial industrial associations at 3.5 per cent. Loans made by provincial industrial associations may not exceed 6.5 per cent; usually 5 per cent; repayment period typically 10 years.

Larger loans from private sources up to SKr1 million ($200,000) eligible for Government guarantees after investigation by provincial employers association and if Labour Market Board considers loan desirable.

Government housing construction loans available for areas of expanding industry.

GRANTS

Belgium:

Government grants available for part of the cost of plant construction and purchase of equipment. Construction grants limited to 20 per cent of costs (30 per cent during recessions); equipment grants to 7.5 per cent of costs (10 per cent during recessions).

Grants normally payable after completion of investment, but an advance of up to 50 per cent of construction grants may be made after roof raised on new plant.

Denmark:

Grants available for the preparation of industrial sites and construction of industrial centers. Grants cover costs of drainage levelling, road construction, and utility installation.

Grants also available for costs of industrial project reviews and analyses, for project preparation, and for other types of consultation.

Local governments offer grants in the form of low-cost building sites and reduced utility charges.

Federal Republic of Germany:

Federal grants may be made for improvement of public facilities. Grants may also be made to nonprofit associations established to improve general economic conditions in a development area, including agricultural improvement and vocational or professional training. The Länder and communities benefiting from the grants must participate in accordance with their ability. Normally a grant is limited to 50 per cent of total cost of a project.

In addition special grants are made to firms located in the border development areas to equalize their freight costs.

France:

Government grants available up to 20 per cent of the total investment costs borne by an enterprise. Investment costs for calculating grants may include new plant construction, new machinery, extension or conversion of existing plants, and transfer of equipment.

One fifth of any grant payable in advance; balance semiannually upon receipt of statement of investment completed.

Government interest subsidies also available for enterprises anticipating only a comparatively low return on investment and borrowing from private sources.

Great Britain:

Government building grants available up to 85 per cent of the difference between the actual cost of plant construction and open market value upon completion.

Government grants also available for other investment costs. Purposes of grants flexible.

Government industrial premises rented to industries at subsidized rates.

Grants to county borough or county district councils toward the cost of acquiring and improving derelict land.

Grants also available for improving basic services in a development area (water, transportation, and so on).

Italy:

Federal government grants may cover up to 20 per cent of the capital needed for establishing new plants or expansion of established plants in municipalities with less than 200,000 inhabitants. Amounts of grant related to cost of building plant, machinery, and equipment and installation of public utilities.

Grants are also offered to cover 100 per cent of costs of public facilities needed for the development of industry and improving productivity in agriculture.

Reduction up to 50 per cent in the freight rates applied for the transport of raw materials and machinery needed for new or expanding plants.

Northern Ireland:

Outright government grants available up to 33.33 per cent of costs of factory construction. Other government grants cover machinery and equipment costs.

Alternate form of aid includes government construction of plants and subsequent rental at reduced rates, together with grants to cover costs of moving machinery and equipment from another industrial site.

Government grants to local authorities for improvements in basic services in industrial districts.

Government grants up to 50 per cent of the cost of training labor for new industrial operations. Alternative is government allowance for worker retraining in Belfast.

Government rebates for part of fuel and power costs.

Sweden:

None provided for industry. Special government grants only to forest owners for extra forest conservation work during seasons of slack employment.

TAX INCENTIVES

Belgium:

Exemption of capital gains tax between 1959 and 1963 provided gains are reinvested in real estate or equipment in regional development areas.

Tax exemptions on up to 30 per cent of profits earned during first three years in a development area.

Five-year real estate tax exemption for enterprises receiving grants or loans for purchase or construction of plants. Local tax concessions also possible for enterprises not receiving loans or grants.

Denmark:

Local governments may use tax exemptions to attract industry.

Federal Republic of Germany:

Accelerated tax depreciation is granted to new industries in border development areas not to exceed $69,000. The accelerated depreciation applies to 30 per cent of the fixed assets and 50 per cent of the movable assets.

France:

Exemption of regional development corporations from 50 per cent of the tax normally due on investment income.

Slightly accelerated amortization on certain forms of plant and equipment acquired after 1950. Fifty per cent accelerated amortization on plant and equipment acquired for research and development purposes.

Deductions may be allowed in certain cases in computing capital gains taxes.

Local taxes may be reduced or eliminated.

Italy:

Exemption from payment of customs duties on imported machinery and materials.

Reduction in registration fees and mortgage taxes to a nominal charge of Lir200. Normal tax on new or extending investment is 7-7.5 per cent of the value of land and buildings.

Fifty per cent reduction of turnover tax on machinery and materials and consumption tax on power used for industrial purposes.

Ten-year income-tax exemption on profits earned in new investment and 50 per cent exemption in taxes on investments in new and additional facilities.

Municipal administrations in southern Italy may grant exemptions from part or all of the taxes they levy.

Northern Ireland:

Local real estate taxes may be reduced by 75 per cent.

SITE IMPROVEMENT AND BUILDING CONSTRUCTION

Belgium:

Development corporations may purchase or build plants in development areas to sell or rent to industries.

Stock of development corporations may be held by national, provincial, or local governments, with proviso that at least one half of total stock must be held by local governments.

France:

Local governments or other organizations may receive governmental aid in the form of loans and interest subsidies for the acquisition and improvement of industrial sites and the construction of plants prior to tenant occupancy.

Great Britain:

Board of Trade may acquire land by agreement or condemnation. Unsightly land may be acquired and improved to permit industrial use or improve neighboring industrial values.

The Industrial Estate Management Corporations acting for the Board of Trade may

1. improve basic services, including water, electricity, and roads;
2. construct plants prior to securing tenants;
3. construct plants to tenant specifications.

Government constructed plants may be sold outright or on deferred terms, or rented to enterprises.

Italy:

Facilities needed for new or expanding plants may be expropriated.

Northern Ireland:

Standard factories between 2,000 and 73,000 square feet constructed by Ministry of Commerce in advance of specific tenants. Government also builds nonstandard factories to manufacturer's specifications in some areas.

Government construction of industrial parks. Land allowance for 100 per cent plant expansion. Industrial park plant extensions made for existing tenants by Ministry of Commerce.

SUGGESTED READINGS

Beveridge, William Henry, *Full Employment in a Free Society* (New York: W. W. Norton & Co., 1945).

Canadian Congress of Labor, Royal Commission on Canada's Economic Prospects, *Probable Effects of Increasing Mechanization in Industry* (Ottawa, 1956).

Cohen, Wilbur J., William Haber, and Eva Mueller, *The Impact of Unemployment in the 1958 Recession*, University of Michigan Survey Research Center, for Special Senate Committee on Unemployment Problems (Washington, D.C.: U.S. Government Printing Office, 1960).

Committee for Economic Development, Research and Policy Committee, *Distressed Areas in a Growing Economy* (New York, 1961).

Devino, William, *Exhaustion of Unemployment Benefits during a Recession* (East Lansing: Michigan State University Press, 1960).

Gallaway, L. E., "Labor Mobility and Structural Unemployment," *American Economic Review*, Vol. LIII, No. 4 (September 1963) 694-716.

Gilmore, Donald R., *Developing the "Little" Economies* (New York: Committee for Economic Development, 1960).

Haber, William, Louis A. Ferman, and James R. Hudson, *The Impact of Technological Change* (Kalamazoo, Michigan: W. E. Upjohn Institute for Employment Research, 1963).

Hancock, K., "Unemployment and the Economists in the 1920's," *Economica*, Vol. XXVII, No. 108 (November 1960) 305-321.

Hart, Albert G., "Measures to be Taken at Different Levels and Distributions of Unemployment," *American Economic Review*, Vol. XLVI, No. 2 (May 1956) 265-274.

Kennedy, Thomas, *Automation Funds and Displaced Workers*, Harvard University, Division of Research, Graduate School of Business Administration (Boston, 1962).

Lebergott, Stanley, "Measuring Unemployment," *Review of Economics and Statistics*, Vol. XXXVI, No. 4 (November 1954) 390-400.

Lester, Richard A., *The Economics of Unemployment Compensation*, Princeton University Industrial Relations Section (Princeton, N.J.: Princeton University Press, 1962).

Long, Clarence D., "Prosperity Unemployment and Its Relation to Economic Growth," *American Economic Review*, Vol. L, No. 2 (May 1960) 145-161.

Moes, John E., *Local Subsidies for Industry* (Chapel Hill: University of North Carolina Press, 1962).

Myrdal, Gunnar, *Challenge to Affluence* (New York: Pantheon Books, 1963).

Nourse, Edwin G., "Ideal and Working Concepts of Full Employment," *American Economic Review*, Vol. XLVII, No. 2 (May 1957) 97-114.

Okun, Arthur M., "Potential GNP: Its Measurement and Significance," American Statistical Association, *Proceedings of the Business and Economic Statistics Section* (1962) 98-104.

Palmer, Gladys L., *et al.*, *The Reluctant Job Changer* (Philadelphia: University of Pennsylvania Press, 1962).

President's Committee to Appraise Employment and Unemployment Statistics, *Measuring Employment and Unemployment* (Washington, D.C.: U.S. Government Printing Office, 1962).

Ross, Arthur M., ed., *Unemployment and the American Economy* (New York: John Wiley and Sons, Inc., 1964).

Somers, Gerald G., *et al.*, eds., *Adjusting to Technological Change* (New York: Harper and Row, 1963).

Thomas, Brinley, ed., *The Welsh Economy* (Cardiff: University of Wales Press, 1962).

United States Bureau of Labor Statistics, Bulletin No. 1264, *Impact on Workers and Community of A Plant Shutdown in a Depressed Area* (Washington, D.C.: U.S. Government Printing Office, 1960).

Bulletin 1368, *Industrial Retraining Programs for Technological Change* (Washington, D.C.: U.S. Government Printing Office, 1963).

The Extent and Nature of Frictional Unemployment (Joint Economic Committee Print, Washington, D.C.: U.S. Government Printing Office, 1959).

The Structure of Unemployment in Areas of Substantial Labor Surplus (Joint Economic Committee Print, Washington, D.C.: U.S. Government Printing Office, 1960).

United States Congress, Joint Economic Committee, *New Views on Automation*, Papers submitted to Subcommittee on Automation and Energy Resources (Washington, D.C.: U.S. Government Printing Office, 1960).

Senate Committee Hearings on Banking and Currency, *Area Redevelopment—1961* (Washington, D.C.: U.S. Government Printing Office, 1961).

Senate Committee on Labor and Public Welfare, *Exploring the Dimensions of the Manpower Revolution* (Washington, D.C.: U.S. Government Printing Office, 1964); *Nation's Manpower Revolution*, Hearings, May–December, 1964 (Washington, D.C.: U.S. Government Printing Office, 1964), 9 Volumes; *Toward Full Employment: Proposals for a Comprehensive Employment and Manpower Policy in the United States* (1964).

Special Senate Committee on Unemployment Problems, *Readings in Unemployment* (Washington, D.C.: U.S. Government Printing Office, 1960).

Universities–National Bureau Committee for Economic Research, *The Measurement and Behavior of Unemployment* (Princeton, N.J.: Princeton University Press, 1957).

Wilcock, Richard C., and Walter H. Franke, *Unwanted Workers* (New York: Free Press of Glencoe, 1963).

ALSO IN THE MODERN ECONOMIC ISSUES SERIES

Economic Growth: An American Problem, edited by Peter M. Gutmann, S-90
The Common Market: Progress and Controversy, edited by Lawrence B. Krause, S-91
City and Suburb: The Economics of Metropolitan Growth, edited by Benjamin Chinitz, S-104

FORTHCOMING VOLUMES

The Economics of Defense and Disarmament, edited by Roger Bolton
The Economics of Poverty, edited by Burton Weisbrod